Especially for

_____

From

_____

Date

_____

Prayers & Promises
for
Times
of Loss

Pamela McQuade

BARBOUR
PUBLISHING

© 2013 by Barbour Publishing, Inc.

Print ISBN 978-1-62416-699-0

eBook Editions:
Adobe Digital Edition (.epub) 978-1-62836-281-7
Kindle and MobiPocket Edition (.prc) 978-1-62836-282-4

Published by Barbour Publishing, Inc., P.O. Box 719, Uhrichsville, Ohio 44683, www.barbourbooks.com

Our mission is to publish and distribute inspirational products offering exceptional value and biblical encouragement to the masses.

ecpa Member of the
Evangelical Christian
Publishers Association

Printed in the United States of America.

Contents

Preface

God brings each Christian many blessings, but none of us can avoid the pain of loss. Since the Fall, humanity has sorrowed over the death of loved ones and struggled to understand why physical and emotional havoc occur.

Losses cause great pain and doubt. Many emotions make up sorrow, but the pain does not end there. Often those of us who grieve struggle with prayer. As our minds race along painful paths or barely seem to function, communion with God can become a sacrifice instead of a simple joy. But because prayerlessness harms spiritual development, we need to make efforts to speak with the Creator.

Those who hurt often need help to focus on one idea at a time or require a starting place for their own prayers. In these pages are petitions, words of thanksgiving, and praises that can act as a starting point for personal prayer or stand alone. However you use them, I hope they will help draw you nearer to the Lord. Each griever who trusts Jesus as Savior can be certain He is close at hand, willing to lift up and encourage the hurting heart that has confessed sin to Him and sought forgiveness. His are the promises in these pages, and He will faithfully keep each one.

Anger

Under Control

" 'The Lord is slow to anger, abounding in
love and forgiving sin and rebellion.
Yet he does not leave the guilty unpunished;
he punishes the children for the sin of
the fathers to the third and fourth generation.' "
NUMBERS 14:18

Hurt that overwhelms makes it easy for us to be angry in everything, Lord. We have less patience with others, situations become stressful, and it's hard to keep life under control.

Thank You for reminding me of Your own nature, which forgave me for so much. Since You want me to become just like You, You call me not to accept quick anger but to avoid all wrongdoing that deserves punishment.

I know I can't do this on my own, so forgive me and fill me with Your Spirit, Lord. I need patience and love in this time of trouble.

Strife

"For as churning the milk produces butter. . .
so stirring up anger produces strife."
PROVERBS 30:33

Loss can bring the worst out in all of us, Lord. When we're under pressure, it's easy to lay blame, pick quarrels with friends, and irritate family members. We're highly stressed, and Satan may try to take advantage of that.

Help me not to stir up anger in others or myself. Your Word promises that as surely as churning milk makes butter, stirring the pot of anger creates problems between people. I don't want to damage tomorrow's relationships because I'm hurting now.

Instead of churning emotions, I need Your peace, Lord. Please turn my heart from sin and pour out Your calm on me so I can live quietly in the midst of trials.

RIGHTEOUS LIVING

∞

Everyone should be quick to listen, slow to speak and slow to become angry, for man's anger does not bring about the righteous life that God desires.

JAMES 1:19–20

You guarantee me, Lord, that my angry words won't get me anywhere I want to go. Spiritual blessings never result from human anger. Though emotion may bend people to my will today, I will pay, long-term, for that emotional shortcut. In the end, I'll wish I had held my tongue.

Help me listen to others, speak carefully, and hold my temper. Though it takes effort on my part, it also brings great benefits.

I want to live to glorify You, Lord, even when I'm hurting. But I can only do that through Your Spirit's power. Fill me today so I can touch my world.

MERCIFUL FORGIVENESS

∾

Who is a God like you, who pardons sin and forgives the transgression of the remnant of his inheritance? You do not stay angry forever but delight to show mercy.

MICAH 7:18

People in pain can generate a lot of anger, Lord. Disappointment, doubt, and fear cause us to strike out at others, even though we know this is not right.

If anger stirs my emotions, remind me of Your forgiveness and mercy, poured out into my heart. Help me grab hold of them and pass them on to others.

I don't want to start a fight and produce bad feelings that last forever, Lord—or even for a while. Instead, I want to forgive and share Your mercy, even when there is still so much pain.

Blessing

GOD AS LORD

*Yes, happy (blessed, fortunate, prosperous, to be envied)
are the people whose God is the Lord!*
PSALM 144:15 AMP

Just knowing You, Lord, is my greatest blessing. Whether life is calm and peaceful or filled with trials, when I rest in You, I am in the right place. Joy, security, and love come from Your hand, and nothing I could buy fills the empty places of my heart as Your Spirit does.

Thank You, Lord, for every blessing you have granted me. Since You care about all of my life, down to the loss of each hair on my head, I live securely. Nothing that happens to me today—or any day—lies beyond Your plan and power. I want to remember that every second of this day.

OBEDIENCE

*All these blessings will come upon you and accompany
you if you obey the LORD your God.... You will be
blessed when you come in and blessed when you go out.*
DEUTERONOMY 28:2, 6

Help me remember, Lord, that when I obey You in the middle of trials, Your blessing follows me wherever I go. Today, as I face a small but difficult task, I could make a decision with long-term impact on my life, so I want to make the right choice.

As I face temptation to make excuses or disobey Your Word, keep me strong in faith, Jesus. Your Spirit's gentle reminder tells me I'm not living just for today but for eternity. Every day of my life, even when I'm hurting, Your blessing of strong faith can cling to me.

PURE HEART

He who has clean hands and a pure heart. . .will receive
blessing from the LORD and vindication from God his Savior.
PSALM 24:4–5

When I'm hurting, it's easy to make excuses, Lord. Often I don't feel like putting in the spiritual effort to fight off sin.

On my own, I cannot ward off evil. Weariness and impatience quickly overcome me, and I find myself trapped in wrongdoing yet again. But as I rely on You alone and allow Your Spirit control over my life, sin is overcome. Focusing on You, I feel temptation's power wane. I have changed by Your power. Your Spirit working in me has cleansed my heart and purified my hands.

Thank You, Lord, for empowering me to do Your will. It's good to know that even in sorrow, I am not destitute.

COMFORT

⌇

"Blessed are those who mourn,
for they shall be comforted."
MATTHEW 5:4 NKJV

I don't really think of mourning as a blessing, Jesus. I'd rather avoid it than embrace it. Yet if I never experienced sorrow, I'd also never feel the comfort that surpasses all this earth can offer. Your love reaches places inside me no human affection can touch. When I've deeply hurt, Your Spirit has consoled me in powerful, unexpected ways.

It's unlikely that I'll ever want to mourn, but when it happens, I know You will stand right with me in the pain. Thank You for healing my heart and giving me relief I can share with others. You alone give perfect peace to the human heart. Thank You, Jesus.

Comfort

GOD'S COMFORT

∾

I, even I, am he that comforteth you.

ISAIAH 51:12 KJV

Lord, I'm so glad that when others oppress me or don't understand my pain, You're still there beside me, lifting me up. With You by my side, I don't fear anything another human can do.

But sometimes it feels hard to turn to You, Jesus. My own doubts and fears interfere. Maybe I worry that You won't understand my situation. Remind me, Lord, that nothing is beyond Your comprehension. You made the earth, our galaxy, and everything that exists—and none of it lies beyond Your understanding.

Help me ask for Your comfort when I need it, Lord. I don't want anything to come between us.

GOD'S SALVATION

∾

Break forth into joy, sing together,
ye waste places of Jerusalem:
for the LORD hath comforted his people,
he hath redeemed Jerusalem.

ISAIAH 52:9 KJV

Even when nothing else brings me comfort, Your salvation consoles me, Jesus. It's not hard for me to imagine where I'd be without Your love—and it would be nowhere good. I wandered in a wasteland before Your love touched me.

Though I struggle now, I know all will eventually work for good. What seems so terrible today will not last forever. Already, piece by piece, positive things are returning to my life. I will never forget my loss, but You bring me new experiences to comfort and cheer or an old truth to remind me of Your love.

Soon I will know Your comfort more completely and will break into a joyous song. My heart's already tuning up for it.

COMFORTING OTHERS

*[God] comforts us in all our troubles, so that we can
comfort those in any trouble with the comfort
we ourselves have received from God.*

2 CORINTHIANS 1:4

I'm glad, Lord, that Your comfort has a purpose. I've learned so much about You in my suffering, and I'd like to pass it on.

All the people who have been there for me, encouraging me when I felt low, have blessed me deeply. I want to give that to others. Help me share Your strength and comfort with anyone who hurts today. You don't give me anything—not even hard times—to hoard.

You've also offered me consolation straight from Your heart, Lord. Even when no one else could help, I felt Your love healing my tenderest spots. Thank You, Jesus, for all Your love. Without it, how would I have made it through?

JOY AFTER A DEATH

❧

For I will turn their mourning into joy, and will comfort them,
and make them rejoice from their sorrow.

JEREMIAH 31:13 KJV

Just as You turned the mourning of Jacob's people into joy,
You've turned my sorrow into happiness again, Lord. I cannot
forget the loved one I lost, but I know You've given me these
years of life as more than a time of extended suffering. There's
still good to do in Your name.

You once saved me from my sins, and now You've delivered
me from overwhelming grief, Lord. Sad living is not what You
had in mind for believers. Blessings for those who love You
have always been Your plan.

Thank You for every blessing in my life, including my days
with the one I love. Help me share this new joy with others
for the rest of my life.

Compassion

With Endurance

~

Indeed we count them blessed who endure.
You have heard of the perseverance of Job
and seen the end intended by the Lord—
that the Lord is very compassionate and merciful.

JAMES 5:11 NKJV

Lord, I know what it is to endure sorrow, but when I look at Job and all his losses, one right after the other, I know my loss is small compared to what some have experienced.

But that doesn't mean my pain is unimportant to You. No matter what I'm going through, if I hold fast to You, Your compassion and mercy find me out. When I suffer and put my faith in Your promises, You always come through.

Thank You, Jesus, that no matter what I may go through, You are still in control of my life, and Your compassion becomes new each day.

Changeless Lord

~

The LORD is gracious and full of compassion,
slow to anger and great in mercy.

PSALM 145:8 NKJV

When I am overwhelmed with grief, it's easy to start questioning You, Lord. *How could this happen?* I wonder, and it doesn't take long for me to start wondering about Your goodness.

I appreciate Your reminding me that though my circumstances have changed, Your eternal goodness cannot. You were good before this occurred, and You remain so throughout the ages. No matter how I'm feeling, Your graciousness, compassion, forgiveness, and mercy work in my life.

Turn aside the doubts that would separate us, Jesus. I want to be faithful to You, no matter how I feel today.

LEAVING THE PIT

[God] redeems your life from the pit
and crowns you with love and compassion.

PSALM 103:4

Though I feel as if I'm at the bottom of a pit, I'm thankful I do not have to stay there, Lord. While sorrow touches my life for a time, You have not given up on me. Your redemption lies ahead, even when my life seems dark.

As I turn to You in all my pain, love and compassion appear new again. Where emotional death once reigned, Your life and joy return. Thank You, Jesus, for pulling me out of the pits of sin and sorrow. Because You gave me new life, I can move beyond the pain and into new joy. In prayer, I'm taking my first step right now.

GOD'S WORKS

∞

He has made His wonderful works to be remembered;
the LORD is gracious and full of compassion.

PSALM 111:4 NKJV

It's easy to get so caught up in my own troubles that I forget Your greatness, Lord. When sorrow fills my heart, the world becomes tiny if I focus on my own pain.

But You have given me so many wonderful things in the world to remind me of Your grace and compassion. Redirect my thoughts again, Jesus, as I am comforted by a child's laugh or the encouragement of a friend. When others remember my loss with tenderness, let it remind me that You love all Your children, including me.

I know You have many more works to do in my life. Keep my eyes open for them as I cling to You now and forever.

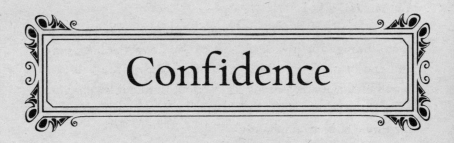

Confidence

In God

*For the L*ORD *will be your confidence
and will keep your foot from being snared.*

PROVERBS 3:26

No matter what my situation, Lord, You promise I don't have to worry about facing sudden disaster. While those who pay You no mind fear the future, anyone whose confidence lies in You remains safe.

I know that doesn't mean I won't face trials, but You promise to go through them with me. Since You know the beginning and end of my life, I can have confidence that You will care for all my in-between needs. Thank You, Lord, for keeping me from being snared. Because I believe in You, Your plans bring me through life triumphantly.

Keep my trust always in You, Jesus. That's where it *should* be. After all, You are my confidence.

The Way of Peace

*The fruit of righteousness will be peace; the effect of
righteousness will be quietness and confidence forever.*

ISAIAH 32:17

When I walk in Your right ways, You promise I can live in quietness and confidence, Lord. My life may not feel that way right now. Confusion seems to hold sway, instead of peace. But

I still trust this is not the way my life will always continue. As I believe in You, even when I cannot see the results of faith, I grow the tree of righteousness. Soon it will flower into quietness and confidence, and my life will be blessed.

Thank You, Jesus, for Your faithfulness to me. When I can't see the path ahead, You point me in the right direction, and I am blessed in Your way of peace forever.

BLESSINGS

∽

"But blessed is the man who trusts in the LORD, whose confidence is in him."
JEREMIAH 17:7

Putting my confidence in You, Lord, can be a challenge. When life seems unhappy and out of control, it's hard to believe. But I haven't put my faith in a mere human who cannot direct my life. My confidence lies in my Creator, who controls all things in heaven and earth. My situation looks small and simple to You, and nothing I face surprises You.

Thank You for giving me this promise to hold on to when my faith weakens. Turn my eyes from my own troubles to You, who has them all under control. Though I may not see it yet, You *are* blessing me. Help me continue to trust that all my ways will be redeemed as I hold on to You.

JESUS, OUR CONFIDENCE

In him [Jesus] and through faith in him we may approach God with freedom and confidence.

EPHESIANS 3:12

Thank You, Jesus, for Your love and willingness to sacrifice Your life for me, enabling me to come to the Father. Without Your shed blood, I'd never experience freedom from sin and would always fear the One who created me.

As Your love brings me confidently into the presence of the Father, remind me that trusting in anything or anyone other than You lands me in a lifestyle of overconfidence in myself. If that were all I had today, pain and loneliness would flood my soul.

I need Your love and guidance for my life. During this trial, strengthen my faith and help me follow confidently in Your way.

Courage

Fighting Discouragement

*"Then you will have success if you are careful to observe the
decrees and laws that the LORD gave Moses for Israel.
Be strong and courageous. Do not be afraid or discouraged."*

1 CHRONICLES 22:13

Discouragement comes easily to me, Lord, when I feel sad.
Sorrow makes me feel so empty inside. It's as if I've lost my
way for a while.

But You remind me that my obedience to Your laws, because
I love You, will give me strength in You. I have no reason to dread.
Just as You were faithful to Moses and Israel, You will keep me,
too.

When I feel weak, Your power can fill me, Jesus. Neither
fear nor discouragement needs to control my heart. You'll win
the fight against fear and depression, if I only trust in You.

Displaced Fear

*"Be strong and of good courage, do not fear nor be afraid
of them; for the LORD your God, He is the One who
goes with you. He will not leave you nor forsake you."*

DEUTERONOMY 31:6 NKJV

It would be so easy to wallow in fear and give up, Lord. But
You've reminded me I am not walking down this frightening
path alone. When You are in charge of my life, I need not dread

what any human can do to me. Even painful emotions flee before Your touch.

Thank You for standing by me, no matter what I face. When I put all my fears in Your hands, I know I am safe. My strength lies in You alone.

Spiritual Courage

"Be strong and very courageous. Be careful to obey all the law my servant Moses gave you; do not turn from it to the right or to the left, that you may be successful wherever you go."

JOSHUA 1:7

When I'm trusting in Your Word—and Your promises to me—I cannot go wrong, Lord. It's only when I turn aside from Your guidance that I fall into trouble again.

Right now I'm not looking for financial success or a promotion. I just need to get through the pain and changes life has brought. Spiritual success means more than physical things. So help me stay on track with You. Help me live to do Your will and feel Your peace again.

Thank You for giving me the courage I need in hard times. I don't know how I'd manage without You, Lord.

WAITING ON GOD

❧

Wait on the LORD; be of good courage,
and He shall strengthen your heart;
wait, I say, on the LORD!

PSALM 27:14 NKJV

It's easy to lose courage when I have to wait, Jesus. If Your Spirit's still, small voice seems silent, doubt may fill my heart. Thank You for letting me know that waiting isn't a sign of Your disapproval. You may be building my heart's strength as I learn to trust in You.

Let my courage remain secure, Lord, even in the quiet times. Even if I'm not doing something "important"—if I don't have a plan and am not taking specific steps to move forward—You may still be doing Your best work in my heart. Thank You for being with me in all things. Help me wait for Your perfect moment with patience, Lord.

Death

God's View

~

Precious in the sight of the LORD
is the death of His godly ones.

PSALM 116:15 NASB

When I'm feeling so sad, it's hard to think about this verse. Right now, death doesn't seem precious to me, Lord, and I hurt to think that the one I love is gone.

Thank You for reminding me that You loved my beloved, too, and rejoiced in that meeting in heaven. You looked forward to the day; then, in a special moment, the two of you met delightedly, face-to-face.

I know death does not mean eternal separation to humans who know You, Jesus. After a time of parting, I'll meet my loved one in Your forever kingdom. Give me strength to wait for Your timing, Lord. Help me finish the mission You have for me here on earth, then bring us together in Your love for all eternity.

Death's End

~

He will swallow up death forever, and the Lord GOD will wipe
away tears from all faces; the rebuke of His people He will take
away from all the earth; for the LORD has spoken.

ISAIAH 25:8 NKJV

One day, You promise, death will exist no longer. Swallowed up, as if it had never been, this great human fear will no longer hold sway over our lives. It's hard to imagine, Lord, since in our temporal world nothing lasts.

I look forward to a tearless day when nothing wicked is in this world, so death no longer has a purpose. When sin no longer grasps at Your people, we can share Your eternal blessings.

Thank You, Jesus, for this promise. When sorrow threatens to overcome me, I know there is still hope. Help me trust in You until that glorious day.

HOPE IN CHRIST

&

For as in Adam all die,
even so in Christ all shall be made alive.

1 CORINTHIANS 15:22 NKJV

How pervasive death is in this world, Lord. No one escapes it, from the plants and animals around us to the people we love most. Since the moment Adam and Eve fell, suffering has been hardwired into our world.

No matter how impossible it is for us to escape death, it still does not have the last word. You sent Jesus to change the world's wiring by overthrowing death and offering life to those who put their faith in Him. The "unchangeable" pattern of death that we could not alter died in a moment of sacrifice, when Your Son gave His life for our sin.

I have no greater hope than this, Lord. I need nothing more. Help me cling to You alone, no matter what I face today.

No Longer Earthbound

∞

"And God will wipe away every tear from their eyes; there shall be no more death, nor sorrow, nor crying. There shall be no more pain, for the former things have passed away."

REVELATION 21:4 NKJV

Every sorrow gone! What a shock that will be, Lord. I can't even imagine what a world without pain would feel like. Such undiminished joy can hardly be thought of on earth.

But I am no longer earthbound. Your Spirit, filling me, offers hope for a new day when I won't even need to cry. Only good things—Your things—will surround me in eternity.

Thank You, Jesus, for placing this hope before me. I need it today more than ever.

Discouragement

STRENGTH IN GOD

∞

Then you will have success if you are careful to observe the decrees and laws that the LORD gave Moses for Israel. Be strong and courageous. Do not be afraid or discouraged.

2 CHRONICLES 22:13

No matter what I face in this world—Lord, with You by my side, I can fend off fear and expect success.

Your promise doesn't come without a condition, though: I must obey Your Word. Only those who trust in You can accept this offer. When I believe that You hold my future and allow Your Word to be my guide, strength and courage will be mine.

Help me cling faithfully to Your Word, Lord. I want to be in the place where You can bless me. Your courage can empower me today.

A COMPANION IN TIMES OF TROUBLE

∞

"Have I not commanded you? Be strong and courageous. Do not be terrified; do not be discouraged, for the LORD your God will be with you wherever you go."

JOSHUA 1:9

Father, those who don't trust in You may pass through times of trouble all alone. But when terror or doubt faces me—like Joshua, I never walk alone.

Thank You for standing by my side through emotional and

spiritual pain, financial woes, or anything else the world can throw at me. Because my life lies in Your hands, You control every part of me—body and soul. You won't sit quietly while I suffer or ignore my physical needs. Every want is cared for when You direct my life.

Walk with me today, Jesus. Fend off the discouragement that aims to overwhelm my heart. I need Your companionship today.

GOD BEFORE US

❧

"The LORD himself goes before you and will be with you;
he will never leave you nor forsake you. Do not
be afraid; do not be discouraged."

DEUTERONOMY 31:8

Where could I go today, Lord, that You have not already been? Could I find a place in this world untouched by Your hand? Have Your feet missed any spot of trouble or blessing?

You promise me Your touch everywhere I go. Whether I'm at work or home, filling out paperwork, or in a court, I need not fear. But my courage doesn't lie in my own abilities or those of my advisors. All my trust is in You, Jesus.

What can I fear when You have prepared my path? Thank You for being there before me, Lord.

GOD'S ENCOURAGEMENT

You hear, O LORD, the desire of the afflicted;
you encourage them, and you listen to their cry.

PSALM 10:17

Even when I feel punished by affliction, You hear the cry of my heart for deliverance, Lord. When I think no one else understands my pain, You seek to lift me up and consider every lament that falls from my heart.

When I'm tempted to feel as if no one cares about me, remind me I'm looking in the wrong place for encouragement. No matter how much friends and family want to help, they are only human. If I doubt Your care, maybe I'm doubting the ability of limited humans to heal my hurts.

Open my ears and eyes to Your encouragement; I need to know You're offering it every day, Jesus.

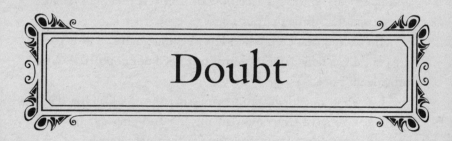

Doubt

A Bright Future

❦

He who goes forth bearing seed and weeping [at needing
his precious supply of grain for sowing] shall doubtless
come again with rejoicing, bringing his sheaves with him.

Psalm 126:6 amp

When I look at my future and things seem black, You remind me, Lord, that You are still in charge of tomorrow, next week, and next year. Nothing I face now or in the years to come has not passed first through Your hand.

Thank You that even when I'm weeping at all I've lost, You are planning a new harvest in my life. I need not doubt You will provide all I need.

Knowing and loving You bring such joy, Lord. One day, I will see Your vast blessings in my life and sing again with delight. Thank You, Jesus, for Your faithfulness and love that keep such promises.

God's Faithfulness

❦

She tastes and sees that her gain from work [with and
for God] is good; her lamp goes not out, but it burns
on continually through the night [of trouble, privation,
or sorrow, warning away fear, doubt, and distrust].

Proverbs 31:18 amp

The light of Your Spirit is never completely extinguished, Jesus, no matter what my predicament. When faith in You burns brightly in my life, I never need to doubt You will bring me good things.

Keep my heart faithful, Lord, even when doubt tempts me and the light burns low. Remind me that Your faithfulness and love never fail.

Thank You, Jesus, for lighting my way into the future. No matter how many dark things surround me, I need never doubt that Your Spirit leads me in the right direction, so my lamp of belief will never go out.

OVERCOMING MOUNTAINS

"Truly I tell you, whoever says to this mountain, Be lifted up and thrown into the sea! and does not doubt at all in his heart but believes that what he says will take place, it will be done for him."

MARK 11:23 AMP

The mountains in my life are not made of rock and dirt today, Lord. Instead they consist of out-of-control emotions, doubts, and fears. But they've become as real as any physical barrier.

I often wonder how to get beyond the obstacles to faith and reach the promise in this verse. You tell me to stand firm, believing despite the troubles surrounding me, and You will toss that mountain into the sea.

Help my doubting heart, Lord. Keep my eyes on You, the unfailing Savior. Remind me that no mountain is big to You, and I've put my faith in the right place.

DOUBTER'S REWARD

*But let him ask in faith, with no doubting, for he who doubts is
like a wave of the sea driven and tossed by the wind. For let not
that man suppose that he will receive anything from the Lord.*

JAMES 1:6–7 NKJV

You promise that doubters get nothing from You, Lord. Those who lack trust receive no reward.

I easily doubt. My limited power in this world quickly convinces me of life's hopelessness. Tossed about by my experiences, not rooted in Your Word, I fail to rely on the one who controls both sea and wind.

When I haven't looked into Your face, I'm really only doubting my own adequacy. Both of us know I can't handle this on my own. Instead I need to turn my eyes to You, recognize Your strength, and cling to You alone. Once I've done that, I have all I need.

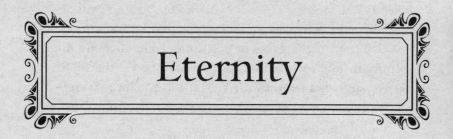

Eternity

One Requirement

~

"For God so loved the world that he gave his one and only Son,
that whoever believes in him shall not perish but have eternal life."

John 3:16

Can it be so simple, Lord? All I must do is believe? It seems easier to add a list of do's and don'ts to faith, but that's not what You require. You promise pure faith opens the door to eternal life.

I'm glad I don't have to jump through hoops to earn Your love. I'm tired of doing that in this world; I'd hardly want it for eternity. In Your compassion, You gave Your Son so that all who believe can spend forever with You. Thank You for that eternal outpouring of love. I never want to be separated from You.

New Life

~

But your dead will live; their bodies will rise. You who dwell
in the dust, wake up and shout for joy. Your dew is like the
dew of the morning; the earth will give birth to her dead.

Isaiah 26:19

Lord, it's hard for me to imagine the day when death will die. No leaves will fall from the trees, there will be no loss of loved ones, no ending of relationships. It all seems too good to be true.

But You are the Father of all good things. You never put us

on earth to die, and You designed eternal life to rise up out of the dust and give birth to the imperishable.

Let me never forget, Jesus, that this world is not all there is. Eternity lies ahead, and I share it with You, if only I've given You my heart. Thank You, Savior, for this never-ending blessing.

BLESSINGS

Jesus answered. . ."Assuredly, I say. . .there is no one who has left house or brothers or sisters or father or mother or wife or children or lands, for My sake and the gospel's, who shall not receive a hundredfold now in this time—houses and brothers and sisters and mothers and children and lands, with persecutions—and in the age to come, eternal life."

MARK 10:29–30 NKJV

I'm amazed by this promise, Lord. Nothing I give up on earth will not be returned, in some way, a hundred times over. On top of that, You offer eternal life.

Right now, I'm feeling disappointed with earthly things. I know they don't last long. They may cause pain and even disaster. So I'm glad I don't only have temporal benefits to look forward to. Thank You for giving me the hope I need: joy in eternity.

MEETING IN JESUS

❧

"I give them eternal life, and they shall never perish;
no one can snatch them out of my hand."

JOHN 10:28

When You grab onto someone, Lord, You promise not to let go. Those who accept Your love cannot die eternally, though death comes to their bodies.

How glad I feel that You offered my loved one life forever. Though separated now, in eternity we will meet again. I have no control over death, but You hold my loved one safely in Your hand. What better place can any of us be in, on earth or in eternity? When You hold us firmly, nothing can destroy us. I know my beloved and I will meet face-to-face again. Together we will worship You forever.

Thank You, Jesus. That's just the security I need today.

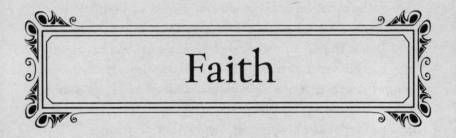

Faith

Real Prosperity

∞

Jehoshaphat. . .said, "Hear me, O Judah and you inhabitants
of Jerusalem: Believe in the LORD your God, and you shall be
established; believe His prophets, and you shall prosper."

2 Chronicles 20:20 nkjv

I think of a lot of things, Lord, when I ponder prosperity. A
job, bank account, or investments signify I am doing well. But
just as the people of Judah could not prosper without knowing
You, neither can I. Faith and blessing cannot be separated.

Thank You for all the good physical things You have given
me. Even in times of trial, don't let me become ungrateful. But
more than that, remind me of the spiritual blessings You've
offered me day by day. Without You I could never know true
peace of mind and heart or experience Your deep love.

Thank You, Jesus, for all these blessings. Help me trust in
You today.

Victory in Jesus

∞

For everyone born of God overcomes the world.
This is the victory that has overcome the world, even our faith.

1 John 5:4

I don't always think of myself as an overcomer, Lord. When
life pushes in on me and things don't go my way, I'm more
likely to feel discouraged than victorious.

Still, faith isn't run by emotions but by Your Word. You've promised that victory is mine, and I can count on that, even on days when it doesn't appear so. Your victory doesn't come because the world works the way I'd like it to. Nor is it related to how many people or things I lose. Victory is mine because You loved me, saved me, and rule in my life today.

When doubt knocks at my door, may my faith answer, saying, "I have victory in Jesus!"

FAITHFUL LORD

But the Lord is faithful, who will establish
you and guard you from the evil one.
2 THESSALONIANS 3:3 NKJV

I have felt the attack of the evil one, Lord, many times in my life. His snares have caught me in sin, and even since You took control of my life, his sneak attacks have tried to lure me away.

But Satan is a defeated enemy, though he attacks often and painfully. When I am strong in You, he cannot bypass Your guard. Though I'd lose the battle on my own, Your strength always defends me successfully. Thank You for protecting me from our enemy, Jesus. No battle that You fight is ever lost.

Speck of Faith

~

So the Lord said, "If you have faith as a mustard seed,
you can say to this mulberry tree, 'Be pulled up by the
roots and be planted in the sea,' and it would obey you."
Luke 17:6 nkjv

Thank You, Jesus, for reminding me that amazing things happen when frail humans exhibit faith. It doesn't take a barrelful of belief, just a tiny bit, like a mustard seed, to start wonderful things in my life and the lives of others.

When even a speck of faith seems hard to come by, Lord, remind me of the One in whom I have belief. In doubt I need only look to You, trust, and ask for help, and You will be with me in a moment.

Thank You for all the amazing things You've done in my life already, Jesus. Help me trust You for more.

Family

Help in Adversity

❧

A friend loves at all times,
and a brother is born for adversity.

PROVERBS 17:17

Thank You, Lord, for giving me family to help me through the hard times. Though we may not see each other often enough, or we may have disagreements or differences of opinion on how each of us does things, when I'm in trouble, my siblings are there for me. It's good to have someone who understands the unspoken needs of my heart and who will help me, no matter what I face.

I appreciate this gift of family that's designed for my saddest days. May it be a blessing to me every hour of my life, in happy times as well as difficult ones. Help me stand by my siblings, too, whatever they're going through in their lives.

God's Family

❧

"Whoever does God's will
is my brother and sister and mother."

MARK 3:35

When I do Your will, I show I'm part of Your family, Jesus. Actions tell more than any words I utter. Just as I don't want to harm my family name by doing wrong, I desire to lift up Your name, even in trials. No one should blame You for my wrong actions; never should anyone think less of You because of me.

When I find it hard to keep up the "family name," remind me I have an older brother to lean on—one who provides for me in all things.

Thank You, Jesus, for loving me enough to make me part of Your family. I want to honor Your name and lead others to do so, too.

Honoring Parents

"Honor your father and your mother,
as the LORD your God has commanded you,
so that you may live long
and that it may go well with you in the land
the LORD your God is giving you."

DEUTERONOMY 5:16

Thank You for this "first command with a promise," Lord. You've outlined a blessing, yet warned me that unless I am good to my parents, the benefits of that blessing will be limited.

It doesn't matter if Mom and Dad were near perfect or far from perfect. You put them in my life for a purpose—and maybe You put me in their lives to reach them with Your truths. Help me to be faithful to You by obeying Your command about how I'm to treat them.

Then, whether I live many years or just a few, I will have lived long in You, and I will be blessed.

HEAVENLY FATHER

∞

"No, the Father himself loves you
because you have loved me
and have believed that I came from God."

JOHN 16:27

You remind me, Lord, that no matter what the state of my earthly family, You remain my eternal Father. When a parent fails me, leaves this earth, or simply can't help me because of earthly limitations, I am not left adrift. You still love me, direct me, and guide my steps.

I'm so glad I'm part of Your family, Father, because You bought my life with Your Son's blood. Though my love is infinitely less perfect than Yours, my feeble response is enough for You. You pour out love on me because I've accepted Jesus in faith.

I have so little to offer, Lord. But what I have is Yours. Thank You for Your love.

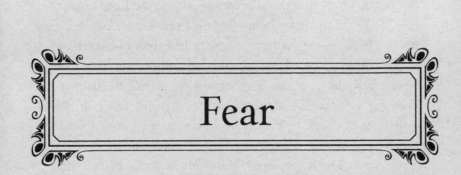

Fear

FEARLESSNESS IN GOD

∞

The LORD is for me, so I will not be afraid.
What can mere mortals do to me?
Yes, the LORD is for me; he will help me.

PSALM 118:6–7 NLT

What do I have to fear when You are on my side, Lord? I know it's true You're there, yet how often do I sense that deep inside my soul? It's easy to doubt when the world comes between us.

When I'm focused on You and faithfully accept Your love, I trust fully in Your power. I cannot be afraid. So help me keep my eyes on You, even when life attempts to get in the way. Turn my heart to Your truths, no matter what this world throws at me.

I love and trust You, Lord. Here's my heart, no matter what doubts I feel.

FEARING PEOPLE

∞

Fearing people is a dangerous trap,
but to trust the LORD means safety.

PROVERBS 29:25 NLT

Being intimidated by people or their works comes so easily to me, Lord. I don't know why others have such power in my life, but their words can make me feel threatened, uneasy, or simply sad. I worry about what they think of me and what they might do to me.

You remind me that my trust should never be in others. People have a limited influence in this world, though I may not recognize it. Forgive me for giving them too much authority in my life.

I know who has the real authority in this world—You do. Help me trust in You instead of wasting energy on fearing people.

SHELTER IN GOD

He will shield you with his wings.
He will shelter you with his feathers.
His faithful promises are your armor and protection.
Do not be afraid of the terrors of the night,
nor fear the dangers of the day.

PSALM 91:4–5 NLT

Day and night, I can trust You, Lord. Whether I go out into the world or stay at home, I am protected by Your love.

Right now I could use a lot of that protection, Jesus. The world seems a scary place because of the loss I've suffered. I never know what to expect and tend to fear the worst, whether I'm facing something new or trying to redesign my old life.

Shield me, O Lord, from my own fears. Give me the trust in You that will bring me through this trial and into deeper faith in You.

FEARING GOD

*"His mercy goes on
from generation to generation,
to all who fear him."*

LUKE 1:50 NLT

Thank You, Jesus, for this promise that I am not the only one to whom You have been merciful. Because I hold You in awe and respect—the proper fear all should have of You—your mercy will follow me and all my family members who trust in You.

No matter how much we hurt right now, we can trust fully in You. You guide and direct us, no matter how deep the pain, and bring us into the peace only Your love can bring.

Pour out Your mercy on us, Jesus. We need it so deeply right now. May we trust in You for everything today.

Finances

God's Gifts

❧

Honor the LORD with your wealth,
with the firstfruits of all your crops;
then your barns will be filled to overflowing,
and your vats will brim over with new wine.

PROVERBS 3:9–10

Jesus, thank You for providing so liberally for me. Your many gifts, spiritual and physical, have filled my life and made it good.

Right now, I may have a hard time seeing that goodness. My aching heart may be blind to Your good things. Turn me again to see that Your love has been with me every day, even in this sorrow. Though trouble faces me today, it will not last forever, and someday Your blessings will shine clearly again.

Open me to sharing these blessings with others—Your peace and grace, the provision I already have, and Your work in my life. Thank You, Lord, for all You give.

Giving

❧

"Give, and it will be given to you. A good measure, pressed down,
shaken together and running over, will be poured into your lap.
For with the measure you use, it will be measured to you."

LUKE 6:38

This is not a time to be stingy, Lord. Thank You for reminding me that others are also in need—some of them much more than

I am. If you have blessed me financially, I need to remember that by giving to others.

You have given me so much, Jesus. Even if I can't offer cash or a large check to someone who's hurting, I have something to give. My time, my faith, and all the other blessings You have given were made mine to share, not hoard.

Help me, even in this situation, to remember others generously. I want to share as You do, Lord.

Fullness in God

≫≪

He humbled you, causing you to hunger and then feeding you
with manna, which neither you nor your fathers had known,
to teach you that man does not live on bread alone
but on every word that comes from the mouth of the Lord.

Deuteronomy 8:3

When I need to rely on You for every bite I eat or every dollar I pay bills with, Your provision becomes very real to me, Lord. I know exactly how You care for me when I see it intimately.

But food is not the only thing You feed me with, Jesus. Your Word costs me nothing, but it offers great blessing. When I meditate on Your promises, my soul overflows with life. In this humbling time, Lord, help me to feed on You. I need to be filled with Your Word today. Nothing else can satisfy.

EVERY NEED

✣

And my God will meet all your needs
according to his glorious riches in Christ Jesus.

PHILIPPIANS 4:19

This promise prompts me to ask, *What do I really need, Lord?* Is there anything I really need that You have not provided?

If I think I'm missing something, let me look again to You. I may not drive the fanciest car, but You have given me transportation—sometimes in the nick of time. You give me a place to live, food, and all the other necessities. If something seems to be lacking in my life, maybe I haven't asked You for it. Or perhaps it's not the best thing for my life, and You are redirecting me.

Even in deep loss, You look out for all my needs. As I come to You, You fill my heart, my soul, and even my pocketbook. Thank You, Jesus, for meeting every need.

Forgiveness

Jesus' Example

〜

If we confess our sins,
he is faithful and just and
will forgive us our sins and purify us
from all unrighteousness.

1 JOHN 1:9

When I look at forgiveness, I look at You, Jesus. Even before I had any idea You existed, You willingly died for me. Though I couldn't have done anything to make You pardon me, Your love prompted You to offer me Your grace.

Help me reflect Your love, Lord, by forgiving those who wrong me. In my own power, I weakly want revenge. But through Your Spirit, poured out in my life, I follow Your loving example.

Forgive me for all my sins, Lord, and make me faithful and pure in You.

Blessed!

〜

"Blessed are they
whose transgressions are forgiven,
whose sins are covered."

ROMANS 4:7

Because my sins are covered by Your blood, Jesus, I am blessed. The wonderful changes You've made in my life have allowed me to see the truth of this promise up close. I'm one who is forgiven, and You've helped me forgive others, too.

No matter what I experience today, Your blessings never alter. You do not change Your mind and decide not to love or forgive me. As I obey You, the good things You offer Your disciples become part of my life.

Thank You for giving me Your blessing, because I need it daily. Help me cling to Your love. No matter what I face, I want to remember that forgiven sin is the most important gift You offer.

GIVING FORGIVENESS

"For if you forgive men
when they sin against you,
your heavenly Father will also forgive you."

MATTHEW 6:14

Because You have forgiven me for so much, You also expect me to forgive others, Lord. The thoughtless remark, the foolish request, the insensitivity of another cannot remain in my heart if I want to obey You, Jesus. You haven't given me a blank check to hold onto the wrongs of others while being forgiven myself. Instead You tell me to take Your love as an example for my life.

Thank You for not holding my sins against me, Lord. Help me forgive those who err against me, too. Make me sensitive to all who hurt me, Lord. Help me love them as You have loved me.

One Savior

"He is the one all the prophets testified about,
saying that everyone who believes in him will
have their sins forgiven through his name."

ACTS 10:43 NLT

No one else can forgive sin, Jesus, as You do. Even before Your birth, the prophets told of Your great mission to planet Earth. Faith in You, they promised, would lead to sin forgiven.

You alone are my Savior, Lord. Though people help or hurt me, they do not command my soul or my salvation. Remind me of this when life becomes too painful or doubtful.

What freedom from sin You brought to me! Nothing on earth gives such cleanness to a soul. Let nothing this side of heaven keep me from faith in You, my Savior.

Friends

CLOSEST FRIEND

A man of too many friends comes to ruin,
but there is a friend who sticks closer than a brother.
PROVERBS 18:24 NASB

Sometimes having many friends seems like a good idea, Lord. When I need help, I'd like to be able to get it wherever I like. But You remind me that too much of a good thing can actually be bad. I can't have close relationships with numerous people at once. Either I get burned out or I will not have time to share honestly.

Thank You for giving me just a few good friends and one Friend who is always there, always ready to help—You. Even when my best friend on earth cannot solve my problems, I go to You and find an answer.

I appreciate Your sticking closer to me than anyone. Help me stay close to You, my best brother.

JESUS, MY FRIEND

"You are My friends if you do what I command you."
JOHN 15:14 NASB

How do I show that I'm Your friend, Lord? You tell me right here: Obedience shows I really love You.

I don't want my faith to be mere lip service. What good is that to anyone? Instead, I need to put belief into action. Your real friends don't just talk about You and Your commands—

they put faith into action every day.

Living faithfully during trials challenges me, Lord, but it also draws me close to You. Our friendship grows in times of trouble as I experience Your trustworthiness and grow in obedience. Being Your friend is more important to me than anything, so help me obey You even when I hurt. You *are* my best friend, Lord.

Friends Like Jesus

He who loves purity of heart
and whose speech is gracious,
the king is his friend.

PROVERBS 22:11 NASB

A pure heart and gracious speech make the right kind of friends—those who love You, Lord. That's the kind of friend worth having, and it's the kind I want, too. But even beyond that, when my heart is pure and I speak with grace, it's because You are my Friend and show me how to touch the hearts of others.

Right now, in times of trouble, I've had some who have shown me their friendship. They've given me help, listened to me, and when doubt threatened, turned my heart to You again. Their pure hearts and gracious speech have comforted my soul. Thank You for their love—and thank You most of all that You have been the Friend who stood by me in the blackest times.

WORLDLY FRIENDSHIP

*You adulteresses, do you not know that friendship
with the world is hostility toward God?
Therefore whoever wishes to be a friend
of the world makes himself an enemy of God.*

JAMES 4:4 NASB

Every time I make a friend, I make a choice, Lord. Will I draw closer to You with a relationship that burns brightly with Your light? Or will I be drawn into the world and far from You?

During times of struggle, it's easy to want the quick fix, to avoid or ignore the pain. Those with slick answers may appeal to me for a time. Remind me, Jesus, that turning from You by making friends with the world ultimately only adds to my pain. Spiritual unfaithfulness will not create a brighter future.

Keep me faithful, Lord, to You and those who love You, too. I want to be Your friend eternally.

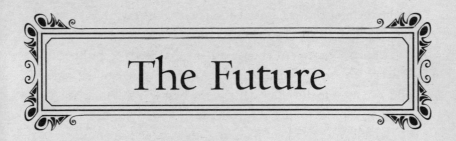

The Future

GOD'S PLANS

"For I know the plans I have for you," declares the LORD,
"plans to prosper you and not to harm you,
plans to give you hope and a future."

JEREMIAH 29:11

When life becomes confusing, I'm glad You have a larger, good plan for me, Lord. When I don't know where to go or how to make the best choices, I need someone to set my path. Lost, I need to find the One who knows the way.

When I can't even choose a road that leads to prosperity, You can. You see the big picture I can't even begin to understand, and You want to direct me daily in the best way. All I have to do is listen, and the route lies before me.

Thank You, Lord, for planning my days and my future.

GOD'S WATCHFUL CARE

The LORD watches over the alien
and sustains the fatherless and the widow,
but he frustrates the ways of the wicked.

PSALM 146:9

Lord, I'm so glad You watch over the weak, the downhearted, and the ones left out by the world. When life feels unfair, it's comforting to know You have not left me. If a wicked person seeks to harm me, You will intervene.

Right now, I feel so powerless, Lord. Help me trust in You for direction for my future. This verse isn't just a line in the Bible—it's a promise of Your care for me. Thank You for caring when I am in trouble. I need Your help right now, Jesus. I'm glad You're watching over me today.

REAL SUCCESS

∞

Commit to the LORD whatever you do,
and your plans will succeed.
PROVERBS 16:3

When the future seems so uncertain, I need to grab onto this promise, Lord. Today, success doesn't seem important, but being able to make a future for myself does. I need to know that things will be all right, that life will hit a new balance, and that I can go on.

Even when I don't consider my future, You do, Lord. That includes more than my financial prosperity. You also have a plan for the spiritual and emotional parts of my life. Though I can't even begin to sort these things out right now, You are already putting them in place in my life.

Thank You for loving me so much, Jesus. Take my whole life now and make it successful in You.

God's Rescue

If the LORD delights in a man's way,
he makes his steps firm;
though he stumble, he will not fall,
for the LORD upholds him with his hand.

Psalm 37:23–24

What a comfort it is, Lord, to know that no matter what I do, when I follow Your way, even my mistakes will be rescued. I may stumble, but I'll never fall flat on my face when I'm in communion with You.

Thank You for helping me avoid trouble and planting my feet on the right path. I'm only human; I still make serious mistakes. Yet even then, You don't desert me. When I'm walking with You, I need fear nothing.

I want to walk together with You for the rest of my life, Jesus. Put me on the path You've designed for me today.

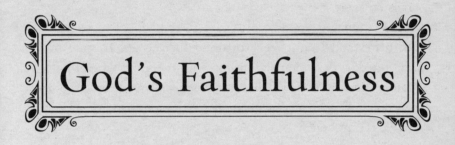

God's Faithfulness

COVENANT LOVE

"Therefore know that the LORD your God, He is God, the faithful God who keeps covenant and mercy for a thousand generations with those who love Him and keep His commandments."

DEUTERONOMY 7:9 NKJV

You are so faithful, Lord. Compared to Your fidelity and mercy, the human capability to stand firm and keep promises falls far short.

I'm amazed You chose to love me and make a covenant with me, and I don't feel worthy of such a gift. Despite my failings, You desired a relationship with me. Even when I have fallen short of Your will and gone against Your Word, You've encouraged me to turn again and keep the commandments You made for my benefit.

Your faithfulness awes me, Jesus. Through Your Spirit, I want to stand as firm in all I do. Help me do that today.

GOD'S CONTROL

Blessed is he whose help is the God of Jacob, whose hope is in the LORD his God, the Maker of heaven and earth, the sea, and everything in them—the LORD, who remains faithful forever.

PSALM 146:5–6

When I need help, I must turn to You, Lord. You make all things in this earth, and You faithfully control all things within this world. Who else should I seek help from when life seems confused and daunting?

Looking to Your creation, I see Your hand in every detail. Thank You for being part of the minutiae of my life, too. When pain fills my heart, You are there, healing me with Your love. If too many decisions face me, You offer Your guidance.

Thank You, Jesus, for all Your blessings of faithfulness. Keep me mindful of them as I seek to trust in You.

CHASED BY BLESSINGS

Trouble chases sinners, while blessings chase the righteous!
PROVERBS 13:21 NLT

I may face trouble today, Lord, but I'm not chased by it every day of my life. Though trials come my way for a while, I more consistently experience blessings from Your hand because I follow You.

Even if I could exist without Your love, I would never want to. Your joy and the blessings You offer are pure delight. No earthly satisfaction could replace Your love. Thank You, my faithful Lord, for generously pouring good things into my life. Spiritually and physically, I have experienced many of Your gracious benefits.

Thank You, Jesus, for keeping this promise. Right now I think I'll turn around and catch a blessing or two.

TRUST IN THE SAVIOR

❧

Give your burdens to the LORD,
and he will take care of you.
He will not permit the godly to slip and fall.

PSALM 55:22 NLT

How I needed to hear these words today, Lord! Though I have put my trust in You, when trials come, it's easy to forget You are in this, too. Yet nothing happens to me that You do not know about, and You are always looking out for my well-being.

Keep my heart firm in this truth, no matter what I face today, this week, and on into the months and years ahead. I want to be firm in faith, trusting only in You, My Savior. Take each of my burdens now, Lord. When Your help is there for me, I don't want to bear them alone.

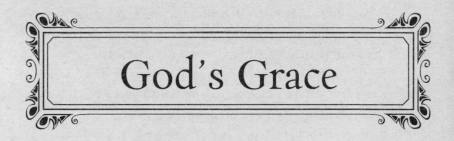

God's Grace

First Grace

～

All have sinned and fall short
of the glory of God,
and are justified freely by his grace
through the redemption
that came by Christ Jesus.

ROMANS 3:23–24

The first, most important step in faith was coming to You, Lord. Before that time, I was caught in sin, desperately falling short of Your glory but unaware there was a problem.

Then You drew me to Yourself, making me aware of Your glory and my sin. You offered redemption. I accepted. From that time, my life has been so different, Jesus.

Without that first step, I would still be lost, unaware of Your love and grace. Pain, not blessing, would fill my days. Thank You, Jesus, for redemption's initial grace, followed by all the others. You have been so generous to me.

Abounding Grace

～

And God is able to make all grace abound to you,
so that in all things at all times, having all that you need,
you will abound in every good work.

2 CORINTHIANS 9:8

When my hands and heart do the right thing, it's because Your grace works in me, Lord. Your blessing, added to my simple efforts, takes an ordinary act and makes it supernatural. With Your love, I touch lives through simple things.

Thank You for pouring out an abundance of grace and blessings in my life. With these, I become Your faithful servant whose works glorify Your kingdom. I am blessed by the grace that causes me to abound in good deeds for You and want to share Your love with everyone I know.

Personal Grace

But to each one of us grace has been given as Christ apportioned it.
Ephesians 4:7

You have given me just the right amount of grace, suited to me personally, Lord. I don't have to be envious of anything another has because Your gift was just for me, useful to glorify You in my own way.

No matter what I'm doing today, You offer grace for all my wants. No matter what my situation, Your tailor-made blessings help me. Nothing in my life is so awful that You cannot bring blessing from it if I seek to do Your will. I need only tap into You moment by moment to experience Your touch of grace.

Thank You for loving me so, Jesus, right down to every detail in my life. Help me do Your will today.

Multiple Blessings

*From the fullness of his grace we have all
received one blessing after another.*

John 1:16

All the good things I receive come from Your hand, Lord, and I should never forget it! How can I avoid this truth if I read Your Word again and again?

I may not see the next blessing on its way. Sorrow has a way of dimming my eyes to life's good things. But when I focus on You again, my vision clears. I remember all the wonderful things You have already given me and Your promises for eternity, and I am glad.

Thank You for never letting me forget how much You love me, Jesus.

God's Mercy

Forever Mercy

∞

Surely goodness and mercy shall follow me all the days of my life:
and I will dwell in the house of the LORD for ever.

PSALM 23:6 KJV

Thanks for reminding me, Lord, that Your goodness and mercy follow me *every* day of my life, not just on happy ones. Though I feel sad, lonely, and doubtful, You still offer me mercy. I want to take hold of it, no matter how life seems to have betrayed me.

I can enjoy Your loving-kindness each day of my life, knowing there's a blessing even beyond the hard days. Help me to focus on the eternity You've promised I will spend with You and to trust that when earth fades away, I'll find myself in heaven with my Savior, whose mercy brought me home.

Thank You for Your goodness and mercy today, Lord. It's just what I needed.

Merciful Blessing

∞

Blessed are the merciful: for they shall obtain mercy.

MATTHEW 5:7 KJV

When I don't feel like extending mercy to family members, friends, or those who flit in and out of my life, I cannot escape this promise, Lord. Some days I'd prefer to give as good as I got, when others do me harm. But Your Word tells me that's no way to blessing—and I've seen that truth in my life.

The struggle to pass Your mercy on to another is worth it, for through giving such grace to others, I receive it myself. Help me pass on Your blessing no matter how I feel. Maybe all I have to do is bite my tongue for a moment in order to be in Your will. Give me the strength I need, Lord, to make Your mercy shine through me.

SALVATION MERCY

God, who is rich in mercy, made us alive with Christ
even when we were dead in transgressions—
it is by grace you have been saved.

EPHESIANS 2:4–5

I wasn't looking for You when Your Spirit first touched me, Jesus. Yet even when I wasn't trying to be bad, sin filled my life. My mind and heart were far from You.

Even so, Your rich mercy called me into Your kingdom. Instead of holding a grudge against me, You brought me to faith through Your Word and the testimony of other believers.

Thank You, Jesus, for giving me that mercy through Your sacrifice. Help me appreciate it every moment of my life and pass that news on to others, too.

MERCY OVER JUDGMENT

For judgment is without mercy to the one who has
shown no mercy. Mercy triumphs over judgment.

JAMES 2:13 NKJV

When I'd like to play tit for tat with judgment, Your Word promises me retribution, Lord. You remind me that if that were the spirit You judged with, I would never spend eternity with You.

You do not triumph through harshly judging us for all our wrongdoing, but in offering mercy to all who will receive it. I need to reflect that spirit when I deal with others. Help mercy to triumph over judgment in my life, Lord. No matter what wrongs have been done me, I want to follow You. Even when it feels very hard, give me victory in You.

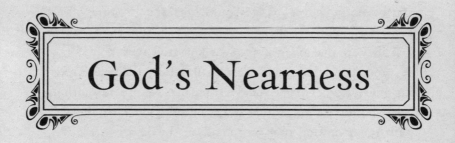

God's Nearness

God beside Me

❦

But you are near, O Lord, and all your commands are true.

Psalm 119:151 NLT

Thank You, Lord, for being near to me even when trouble stands on my other side. Nothing, not even all this world's pain, could be closer than You.

Thank You, Jesus, for this double promise that You always stay by me and never change Your truths. Your promises of care and protection never alter. They were true before I experienced loss, they are true today, and they will be true forever.

Your faithfulness and nearness in all my trials deserve all my praise, Lord. No one stands by me like You. There's nothing You won't do for me as long as I'm faithful, too. Help me walk with You, following Your commands all my days.

Space between Us

❦

Come near to God and he will come near to you. Wash your hands, you sinners, and purify your hearts, you double-minded.

James 4:8

When I feel as if you stand far from me, Lord, it's not that You distanced Yourself from me. *I* moved. Though I might not have lifted my feet, gotten on a train, or flown anywhere, I traveled far from You in my thoughts and actions. Suddenly, You seemed miles away.

I don't want to live a millimeter farther from You than I

need to, Jesus. Space between us is a terrible idea. So when my hands and heart are anything but clean, turn me to plunge them again in Your blood, asking forgiveness for my wrongs.

Thank You, Jesus, for wanting me near, despite my lack of perfection. Nothing is better than being close to You.

CALLING IN TRUTH

The LORD is near to all who call upon Him,
to all who call upon Him in truth.
PSALM 145:18 NKJV

All I have to do is call on You, being really interested in knowing You and Your ways, and You are near, Jesus. I don't have to jump through hoops or achieve some kind of personal perfection, just have an open heart.

Thank You for wanting to stand next to me, though my heart and mind are confused. Though people desert me or cannot be beside me, You are never put off by my problems.

Make my heart tender toward You, Lord, so I can daily call on You in truth instead of setting my own agenda. I need You near; may Your Spirit fill my heart as I call on You now.

Shelter in Him

Those who live in the shelter of the Most High
will find rest in the shadow of the Almighty.

Psalm 91:1 NLT

What a picture of closeness this is, Lord! How far could I
be from You when I rest in Your shadow? Could I find a better
place to live than in Your shelter? There I lack for nothing. You
house me in many blessings because I am at Your side.

I want to live in Your place, Lord, and share the blessings
of Your rest. Peace, love, and harmony fill my life as I stand by
Your side. You offer me every good thing, simply for sticking
close to You. May I always find my rest in You, Lord. Show me
how to live in Your shelter today.

God's Plan

Before Birth

~

Your eyes saw my substance, being yet unformed.
And in Your book they all were written, the days fashioned
for me, when as yet there were none of them.

Psalm 139:16 NKJV

Even before I was born, You knew just what every day of my life
would be like, Jesus. I can barely take this truth in!

The fact that nothing that happens to me is a surprise to
You gives me comfort. Though I may face days that seem out of
control, I need to remind myself I need not worry. Nothing in
this life is beyond Your authority. Even when life seems dark,
unfair, and evil, You have not yet had the last word.

Your greatness humbles me, Lord. Beyond all things, I
want to glorify You.

In Control

~

But the LORD's plans stand firm forever;
his intentions can never be shaken.

Psalm 33:11 NLT

My plans change from day to day, so it's hard to imagine that
Yours are immutable, Lord. But I'm glad nothing alters with
You, because I need a Rock to stand firm on.

When my life skittles about like a bug on water, it's good to
know You still have a blueprint for life that no one and nothing
can overthrow. I may not see Your design or even appreciate it

for a while, but Your strategy still leads my out-of-control life to victory.

With my life in Your hands, I need never fear my own loss of control. As You direct a life, it always comes to perfect completion. Jesus, thank You for Your unchanging love.

GOD'S PURPOSE

∽

You can make many plans,
but the LORD's purpose will prevail.
PROVERBS 19:21 NLT

Right now, my outlook seems kind of vague, Lord. The future seems unpredictable because my mind is on overload. The choices I have to make overwhelm me at times. Not knowing what plans to form or how they will turn out causes me to struggle.

At this moment, I put all my strategies in the best place—Your hands. Take control of everything I do and say. Show me Your purpose in my life or guide me in the right direction, even though I cannot understand.

I need Your design to guide my days because I want Your purpose to prevail. Achieve Your goals in my life, Lord.

PERFECT PLAN

❧

God had planned something better for us so that only
together with us would they be made perfect.

HEBREWS 11:40

Your plan of salvation included both Jews and Gentiles, Lord. Old Testament predictions were fulfilled in Your Son, Jesus, on the cross. Together, all who believe are brought under Your blood.

We have yet to see the very end of the plan, when You come in glory and reestablish Your throne, but we know it will happen as surely as You sent Your Son. So many are Your fulfilled promises that we hardly have reason to doubt.

I know You also have wonderful things planned for every day of my life, based on Your Son's work. Help me look to Your plan when life seems less flawless than I'd imagined. In the end, I know You can redeem all this.

God's Protection

His Rescue

"Because he loves me," says the Lord,
"I will rescue him; I will protect him,
for he acknowledges my name."

Psalm 91:14

Those who love You are rescued by You, Jesus! What a wonderful promise.

I've seen it, Lord, when I was in trouble through no fault of my own and You sent me unexpected help before I could even ask. But other times, I've intentionally claimed this promise and seen You come through. Thank You for Your faithful love.

Now I need Your rescue from suffering, faithful Lord. Though my situation may not change, you can make a change in me. Work in my life, complete Your process of reclamation, and make me holy in You.

Justice in Jesus

He guards the paths of justice
and protects those who are faithful to him.

Proverbs 2:8 nlt

Right will win out, no matter what I'm experiencing today, Jesus. I can count on Your promise to guard justice and protect me because I've been faithful to You.

It doesn't always seem like that when I'm in the middle of a trial. Because I can't see into the future to understand Your final plan, I may worry that right will not be done. Help me trust in You, even when justice seems distant. Keep me faithful to You, no matter what situation lies before me.

Thank You for keeping me from harm and bringing good even out of my troubles. I trust in You for all things, Lord.

SURE CHOICE

❧

Seek his will in all you do,
and he will direct your paths.
PROVERBS 3:6 NLT

Decisions don't always come easily to me, Lord. I may peer into the future, wondering if an alternative will turn out right or wrong. In my own power, I'm clueless. But You haven't left me on my own, helpless in the face of choice. Instead, You promise that if I heed You, You'll guide my path in the right direction. That hasn't meant I've never made a mistake. But somehow, in the long run, as I've listened, I have ended up on the path that glorifies You.

When grief overwhelms me, I need Your clear direction. Show me surely how to make the wisest decisions in this time of trial, and lead me always in Your way.

God's Sheltering Arms

*The LORD is a refuge for the oppressed,
a stronghold in times of trouble.*

PSALM 9:9

I always need Your shelter from life's storms, Lord, but sometimes I seek shelter more often because of the challenges I face. When hurts go deep, I need a place of understanding and love.

Thank You, Jesus, for sheltering me when the world pushes in and seeks to wring all joy from my life. When I receive new life from You, I go out into the world again, strong in commitment. As Your love lives within me wherever I go, Your shelter remains with me, guarding my heart in You. You are the only protection I need.

Guidance

IN THE RIGHT DIRECTION

*He guides the humble in what is right
and teaches them his way.*

PSALM 25:9

Thank You, Lord, for letting me know I don't need a certain worldly status or stature to live in Your kingdom. You aren't seeking the famous or learned, just anyone who will humbly look to You for direction. When I come to Your side, willing to listen to Your counsel, You set me on the glory road.

I can't imagine living without Your guidance. You've set a challenging path before me, yet depending on You brings great joy. So many blessings come from living for You that I wouldn't want any other lifestyle.

Please show me all I need to know today and lead me in the right way. I don't want to set foot on any path but Yours, Jesus.

THE BEST ROUTE

*I will instruct you and teach you in the way you should go;
I will guide you with My eye.*

PSALM 32:8 NKJV

You haven't left me wandering in a wilderness of sin, Lord, but showed me the way to Your kingdom. Thank You for placing me on a new path and daily offering guidance for each confusing moment and every trouble.

I'm so glad You don't expect me to figure out some difficult road map. When it comes to doing Your will, Your Word offers clear direction to all who seek it. You never fail those who seek to follow You faithfully.

Because You always watch over me no matter where I go, Jesus, let every path I take be one that pleases You.

PERFECT COUNSELOR

"However, when He, the Spirit of truth, has come,
He will guide you into all truth; for He will not speak on
His own authority, but whatever He hears He will speak;
and He will tell you things to come."
JOHN 16:13 NKJV

Sometimes, Lord, I wonder whom I can turn to in trouble. When I seek the advice of many and simply end up more confused, it may be because I haven't first turned to the perfect counselor—You.

I'm not saying I don't need advice from wise people You've put into my life, but even the best human won't always know how to counsel perfectly. No one can direct my paths the way You can, Lord.

Thank You, Jesus, for giving me Your Spirit's direction. Help me seek You first and walk in Your counsel all my days.

Path of Blessing

∞

All the paths of the LORD are mercy and truth,
to such as keep His covenant and His testimonies.

PSALM 25:10 NKJV

Keeping Your Word brings mercy and truth into my life, Lord. Who would want to live any other way? How can multitudes bypass Your best blessings? It's a mystery to me.

How can I thank You for calling me to live in Your blessings, Jesus? Though keeping Your Word every day challenges me, so many blessings come from doing Your will.

Even if I fail, Your mercy draws me back to Your way. Your never-failing love does not leave my heart. But I don't want to wander from Your side, Lord. Make me faithful to You every day.

Healing

FOR RIGHTEOUS LIVING

❧

[Jesus] Himself bore our sins in His own body on the tree,
that we, having died to sins, might live for righteousness—
by whose stripes you were healed.

1 PETER 2:24 NKJV

First, You healed my spirit, Jesus, and then You gave me a new life focused on righteous living instead of my own failures and sins. Your immense sacrifice, which I believed in, caused my complete change of heart and attitude.

No matter what I'm going through today, that truth has not changed. I'm not the person I was before Your Spirit entered my life and broke sin's grip on me. Though I struggle with day-by-day temptations, sin no longer directs my future. Help me live for You no matter what life brings my way today. I don't want anyone to think Your healing will not last.

BODY AND SOUL

❧

"If you diligently heed the voice of the LORD your God and do what
is right in His sight, give ear to His commandments and keep all
His statutes, I will put none of the diseases on you which I have
brought on the Egyptians. For I am the LORD who heals you."

EXODUS 15:26 NKJV

Your regeneration touches my life in many ways, Lord. First, You drew me to Yourself in love, healing all my sins. Since then Your ongoing reconstruction project works in all my life.

As I obey Your commands, I avoid so many horrors, Jesus. Spiritual maladies cannot touch me when I live faithfully in Your Word. I even avoid some physical illnesses as I bypass wrongdoing that affects body as well as soul.

Thank You for healing all of me, Jesus. I need You in every corner of my life.

MEMORY HEALING

He heals the brokenhearted
and binds up their wounds.
PSALM 147:3 NKJV

No one can wrap a bandage around a heart, Lord. In this world, it can't be done. But Your Spirit performs its healing work every day, reaching into places no human can touch.

Thank You for binding up my grief as I've trusted in You. Though sorrow still lingers, You have begun to make my memories sweet. Even in the worst of situations, You've brought good remembrances to my mind and heart. I give my life to Your powerful touch, Lord. Reach into the still-painful places of my heart and teach me to trust in You for all things.

End of Mourning

"I have seen his ways, and will heal him;
I will also lead him,
and restore comforts to him
and to his mourners."

ISAIAH 57:18 NKJV

You are rebuilding my life, Lord, though I've been through great sadness. Once, I could not believe life would be worth living again, but You have renewed my joy and purpose.

Thank You, Jesus, for watching over me during this grief, for directing me, even when I was so confused I didn't know where I was going. My life has been permanently changed but not destroyed. Still, You are working in me, offering me blessings I had doubted existed.

Take the rest of my days, Lord, and make them profitable to You and Your kingdom. There is so much more to life than I'd imagined—especially life in You.

Joy

Future Joy

Weeping may go on all night,
but joy comes with the morning.

PSALM 30:5 NLT

Even when grief seems overwhelming, Lord, You encourage me to believe it will not last forever. My mind knows sorrow has an end, though my pain-filled heart feels it will never heal.

While I can't imagine joy, You look out for my future, preparing good things I can't perceive in the depths of my sorrow. When I cannot look ahead, You do it for me.

I can't thank You enough, Jesus, for watching over me; heading me in the right direction, even when I'm blinded by grief; and looking ahead, to create joy for me on earth and in eternity. Thank You for putting joy in my future. One morning, it will flood my soul.

Heart's Desires

Take delight in the LORD,
and he will give you your heart's desires.

PSALM 37:4 NLT

Delighting in the world gives me only emptiness, Lord. In my grief I know that, because things can't take the place of my loved one. Whether I have much or little, it cannot replace the joy we shared together.

But when I delight in You, You fill even the hurting places,

Jesus. My grief doesn't end in a moment, but You walk through it with me and begin the healing process. In moments of pain, Your kindness has lightened my heart.

Keep my heart close to You, Jesus. I love to feel the touch of Your love and enjoy close fellowship with my Savior. When I'm near You, my heart never feels empty.

JOYFUL

∞

You will show me the path of life;
in Your presence is fullness of joy;
at Your right hand are pleasures forevermore.

PSALM 16:11 NKJV

Before I knew You, Jesus, I never thought of finding joy in God. Those who don't love You can't understand the pleasures of Your Spirit. Once Your light shone on me and I accepted Your gift of new life, You became my greatest delight.

Keep me mindful of the joy to be found in You, Lord, when the world seems dark and doubtful. As trials turn my focus away, may Your Word remind me of the fullness of joy I've had with You.

No matter how sorrowful this world seems, You store up eternal pleasures I can share with You. Keep me walking in the light of Your path, pleasuring in the earthly joys You give until we share eternal bliss.

Sorrow's End

〜

So the ransomed of the LORD shall return,
and come to Zion with singing,
with everlasting joy on their heads.
They shall obtain joy and gladness;
sorrow and sighing shall flee away.

ISAIAH 51:11 NKJV

One day, all sorrow shall end, just as You promised, Lord. Time will cease in a flood of joy as You complete salvation. Now, as grief floods back on me, I look forward to that day. I'd like to see an end to the pains I've felt on earth.

Constant, unrestrained joy in You is unfamiliar to me, Jesus. Used to the sorrows of this world, I can hardly imagine what it will be like. But I trust I'll know it in eternity. Living with and delighting in You forever will make my heart sing.

Help

Faithful Promises

∞

Every word of God is pure; He is a shield
to those who put their trust in Him.

PROVERBS 30:5 NKJV

You don't make unsubstantiated promises, Lord. I know that. Those who wrote down Your promises in scripture didn't make mistaken pledges for You; every word faithfully represents Your will and Your being. So when You say You'll be my shield because I've trusted in You, I can take You at Your word.

When trials attack, I need to stand behind You, Lord, instead of running ahead and seeking to make my own defense. I trust You, Lord, to provide all the help I need whenever I face trouble. Be near me, no matter what I experience today. Whatever You give me, it will be right.

Delivered!

∞

For he will deliver the needy who cry out,
the afflicted who have no one to help.

PSALM 72:12

When I feel helpless, I'm really not, Lord. No one who has Your aid is alone and without support.

Not only do You stand beside me when I'm in trouble or pain, You promise to deliver me. Whether I need financial, spiritual, or emotional help, You provide all I require. The only reason I could lack anything I truly need, Jesus, is that I've forgotten to ask You. Keep me in devoted connection with You, sharing every need, and I will never be needy or lost in affliction.

Thank You, Lord, for caring for all my needs and hurts. You are always faithful to me.

Helped

∞

And the Lord shall help them and deliver them...
because they trust in Him.
PSALM 37:40 NKJV

I've felt weak, Lord. Emotionally and physically, I've learned what it's like to barely be able to cope with life. But even in the midst of trouble, You have pulled me through. Others have joined hands to help me, and somehow even the biggest problems have begun to work themselves out. I know it's not because I've done such a great job—You have been smoothing the way for me.

Thank You for delivering me from trouble at just the right moment. You are so great, Jesus, I can't begin to offer You enough thanks. But I appreciate every scrap of help You've given.

Refuge and Strength

∞

God is our refuge and strength,
a very present help in trouble.

PSALM 46:1 NKJV

When I don't know where to turn, Lord, You remind me You are always my refuge and strength. If I need a safe place to hide from the world for a time, You are there.

But I appreciate that You don't let me avoid reality for long. Instead You offer real help—strength to return, strong and vibrant, to take on every challenge. With You by my side, I will not hide from life but reenter it with the ability to overcome every trouble.

Thank You for giving me the assistance I need to go on. Your help returns me to life the way I should live it—focused on You alone. Help me rely on Your strength in every trial.

Hope

GOD'S REDEMPTION

∽

*O Israel, put your hope in the LORD, for with the LORD
is unfailing love and with him is full redemption.*

PSALM 130:7

Thank You, Jesus, for Your unfailing love that reached down
and drew me in. I've learned that Your saving work didn't touch
me for only a moment; it reclaimed every second of my life—
even the bad ones. Whatever trials I pass through, You remain
beside me, working out Your total redemption. Hope need not
wait for eternity; it's evident in my daily experiences.

Help me to faithfully trust in You, Lord. In nothing else
will my future, through eternity, be bright.

UNDISAPPOINTED

∽

*Now hope does not disappoint, because the love of God has been
poured out in our hearts by the Holy Spirit who was given to us.*

ROMANS 5:5 NKJV

I have a reason to hope, Lord, unlike so many in this world.
Those who trust in a vague, happy future or have unfounded
optimism lack the one thing they need—Your Spirit in their
hearts.

Only Your Spirit, working in love in my life, never fails.
Knowing You means that a frail human need not give in to the
pressures of life's negative impacts. I need not fail when Your

love strengthens my fainting heart.

Thank You for the hope that never disappoints, Jesus, for whenever I hope in You, I'm putting my heart in the right place.

WRITTEN HOPE

For whatever things were written before
were written for our learning,
that we through the patience and comfort
of the Scriptures might have hope.

ROMANS 15:4 NKJV

When my heart begins to fail or doubt knocks at my door, You have not left me without counsel, Lord. No matter how the world attacks, the scriptures record Your love, hope, and guidance.

Thank You for giving me Your Word to encourage me when I feel down. Strengthen me in the face of doubt, and lead me in Your perfect way. Without Your Word in my heart, life would become dark, dreary, and incredibly painful. But Your truths heal my heart and teach me how to live in hope.

Help me learn more of You, Jesus, throughout my days. I never want to lose the hope You offer.

ENCOURAGED!

∞

Be of good courage, and He shall strengthen your heart,
all you who hope in the LORD.

PSALM 31:24 NKJV

Where can I find strength to go on in trials? Only in You, Lord. When my heart falters and I cannot imagine where to turn, I lift my face to You and suddenly receive the energy to go on. Your Spirit leads me in the right direction, even when every map and compass seem to fail.

Other paths only seem to offer hope. For a while I might feel encouraged, but no other faith, no human or physical solution, has Your eternal strength. Everything humanity comes up with falls short of Your heart-empowering ability, Lord.

Thank You, Jesus, for lifting me up. I need Your courage filling my life if I'm to live for You.

Loneliness

Never Alone

❧

I will pray the Father, and he shall give you another Comforter,
that he may abide with you for ever; Even the Spirit of truth...
[who] dwelleth with you, and shall be in you.

John 14:16–17 KJV

Loss makes me feel so lonely, Lord. You gave me my loved
one as a great blessing, but this hole in my heart seems so large.
Nothing takes the place of that relationship—and honestly, I
wouldn't want anything in that spot in my heart. Those we love
can never be replaced.

You've promised comfort to those with Your Spirit inside.
Though no one takes the place of my beloved, Your Comforter
offers strength, healing, and peace. I need those now, Lord, to
fill my empty places.

Make my heart new in Your Spirit, Jesus. With You, I never
need be alone.

A Large Family

❧

God places the solitary in families and gives
the desolate a home in which to dwell.

Psalm 68:6 AMP

When I feel lonely, Lord, remind me that You've given me a
family. It may not be as perfect as I'd like, but having one reminds me You care for me as a child and want me to fellowship
with others.

Even if my blood relatives cannot be there for me, You've sent me an even larger family, filled with those who love You. My brothers and sisters in Christ span the globe, and some reach out in love to me. With so many siblings, I am never really alone.

Thank You for caring even for my loneliness, Lord. Fill it with people who love You.

TRUST IN GOD

❧

In peace I will both lie down and sleep, for You, LORD, alone make me dwell in safety and confident trust.

PSALM 4:8 AMP

Because I can rest assured You are caring for me, I sleep peacefully, Lord. I need not keep myself awake nights, worrying about my life, relationships, or future troubles. If I wake, I can turn to You in prayer and receive comfort from You. No matter what happens, You guard me and keep me from harm.

Thank You, Lord, for giving me Your rest and peace, despite the troubles I have faced. When I'm connected to You, Jesus, I have nothing to fear!

Tapped into Jesus

"I am the vine, you are the branches; he who abides in Me, and I in him, he bears much fruit, for apart from Me you can do nothing."

John 15:5 nasb

Abide in You! How often I forget to do that, Lord, when trials rise up in my face and confusion rules my life. It's easy to forget I'm not alone and don't have to handle things single-handedly. As I handle things on my own, I often feel left out, lonely.

I want to be tapped into You, Jesus, every moment of my life. May nothing I do be separated from Your will. Connecting to You brings me many blessings—not the least of which is the joy of Your amazing love. Let me ever be Your branch, O Lord.

Loss

Nothing's Lost

"Whoever finds his life will lose it, and whoever
loses his life for my sake will find it."

MATTHEW 10:39

When I find my life in You, Lord, nothing important can be completely lost. Even loved ones who die, if they believe in You, will meet me again in eternity. Anyone believing in You can never be truly lost again. Trials may come, testing faith, but nothing separates us from Your love and the promise of eternity. Once You've written *found* on our lives, it can never be erased.

But here on earth, Jesus, I often experience and fear loss—this side of heaven, people and things can be close to me and much valued. Remind me always that this world is temporary. Only what I hold in You lasts forever. I want my life to reflect that truth as I cling only to You.

Tiny Steps

"And if anyone gives even a cup of cold water to one of these
little ones because he is my disciple, I tell you the truth,
he will certainly not lose his reward."

MATTHEW 10:42

Whatever I do, whomever I love, no good thing is wasted if I'm doing Your will, Jesus. You've promised that even the smallest act, done out of love for You, reaps an eternal reward.

Right now my frail spirit may only be capable of small acts of kindness. Don't let that weakness deter me from speaking the encouraging word or doing the small, kind deed that springs from faith. Tiny steps now may lead to large ones later.

How often have little acts, done by others, lifted my sad spirit and reminded me to trust in You? Help me reach out to others who need that message now.

GOD'S GRASP

"And this is the will of him who sent me,
that I shall lose none of all that he has given me,
but raise them up at the last day."

JOHN 6:39

Because I'm Yours, Lord, chosen for eternity, I live in confidence that even serious loss can never steal my most important treasure. Your grasp on my soul is not so weak that anyone or anything can part us.

I may lose many temporal things. You've never promised homes or bank accounts will remain. They're given to me only to use for a while to benefit Your kingdom.

But any heart You hold, You keep forever, firm in Your hand. In eternity, I—and all who put their faith in You—will be lifted up into an infinity of praise and worship for You alone.

Thank You, Lord, for holding to me tightly in love.

God's Fullness

"The thief comes only to steal and kill and destroy;
I have come that they may have life, and have it to the full."

John 10:10

You do not give me emptiness and loss, Jesus, but a life full of You, overflowing with blessings. As I resist sin and give You control of my life, Your Spirit overflows in me.

With You, painful, empty times cannot last. Though they linger awhile, they cannot permanently defile the place where Your Spirit works. Though I suffer loss, You do not destroy me. Instead, You are emptying me out to build new things in my life and head me in a different direction.

I do not enjoy loss, Lord, but I rejoice that even from this You bring a new, blessed life. Take control of me today, and make me full in You.

Love

THE PATIENCE CHALLENGE

Love is patient, love is kind.

1 CORINTHIANS 13:4

My loving isn't always patient, Lord. Even trying to love myself rightly, in the face of failure, I quickly run into a block of impatience. When others challenge my ability to love, patience becomes even more difficult.

But You are always patient, kind, and caring. Your love never flags. Even when I haven't deserved it, You've offered me second chances and moments of repentance.

That kind of attitude, offered to the world, can change lives if I pass it on. I want to reflect Your love, poured out so generously on me. Though I may not feel I do it well now, I want to become patient. Help me grow in Your patient love, beginning today.

DELIGHTED LOVE

Rather, the LORD's delight is in those who honor him,
those who put their hope in his unfailing love.

PSALM 147:11 NLT

You delight in me, Lord. What a wonderful thought! There aren't a lot of people in the world who find delight in me—a few precious ones, but every one is special. How much more wonderful that the Lord of heaven and earth loves me this way.

As I treasure Your love, may I also never take it for granted.

It's easy to take advantage of those who love me, and I don't want to fall into that trap. I want to honor You all of my days and bring You joy daily. Knowing You never fail me should make that easy, yet sin still invades my best intentions.

Keep me mindful of Your faithfulness to me so I can be faithful to You, too.

Faithful in Trials

❧

"I am the LORD, I am the LORD, the merciful and gracious God. I am slow to anger and rich in unfailing love and faithfulness."

EXODUS 34:6 NLT

How often, Lord, I've heard others grumble about how hard life is or even blame You for wrongs in this world. Have they read this verse and trusted in Your love? Probably not.

Though I know You and experience Your love, when life becomes challenging, I'm tempted to think the world has gone awry and wickedness has won. It's not true, of course. This promise of Your nature, so large and unfailing in love, has never been destroyed, even if You don't act as weak humans expect.

Though trials come, keep me mindful of Your unchanging mercy and graciousness, poured out even in the worst situations. Help me see Your work, Jesus, in everything on earth.

ENDURING LOVE

Give thanks to the God of gods.
His faithful love endures forever.

PSALM 136:2 NLT

What can stop Your faithful love, Lord? Nothing on earth or in heaven, because no one and nothing is greater than You. If You seem far away, it isn't because You moved.

If Your touch seems distant, help me trust in You, turning from sin to faith. Thanks—not complaints—should fill my life as I rely on Your love to bring me through. Our communion swells again, and I feel Your love.

Keep me faithful and thankful in all my trials, Lord. Help me cling to Your powerful love and draw near to You. Nothing else will fill my heart with joy.

Thank You, Lord, for Your unending love.

New Life

Glad Life

❦

The humble shall see [God's salvation] and be glad;
and you who seek God, your hearts shall live.

Psalm 69:32 nkjv

New life in Your salvation! I felt Your touch, Jesus, and joy filled my heart. But You never meant that delight to last a moment and fade. Your joy should be an everlasting theme in my daily living.

Trials often begin to squeeze gladness from my life. Overwhelmed, I feel doubt slip in and wonder what went wrong. But trouble doesn't have to rule my days. Thank You for the promise, Lord, that if I humbly turn and draw closer to You, joy will reignite.

Jesus, draw me near today. Your new life fills my heart, even in troublesome times.

Resurrection Power

❦

"I am the resurrection and the life. He who believes
in me will live, even though he dies."

John 11:25

Living even though we die is a strange concept to us humans, Lord. Death and life seem so black and white. When we lose a loved one, emotional pain darkens our lives and makes death seem somehow permanent. But You're reminding me it isn't. Those who trust in You during their earthly years experience

Your resurrection in their own changed lives. Death doesn't end the resurrection process. It simply completes it.

If beloved ones knew You, I can count on our meeting again in eternity. You, the resurrection and the life, will draw us to Yourself and let us share eternity in Your glory.

Thank You, Jesus, for this final blessing. Give me faith to trust I'll see those I love in our final home.

COMPLETELY NEW

∽

We were therefore buried with him through baptism into death in order that, just as Christ was raised from the dead through the glory of the Father, we too may live a new life.

ROMANS 6:4

Just like You, Jesus, the faithful dead will be raised to new life. We've seen a reflection of that coming new life in our death to sin, through baptism. Symbolically, all our wrongs were swept away in water, and we entered into Your new life.

But faith in You is not only for eternity. Every day, I live newly, putting aside sin and sharing Your promise with those still dead in sin. I cannot rest on a one-time act to claim a place in heaven. Help me make Your new life a reality through my daily faithfulness to You. Then, when I reach heaven, I will be entirely new in You.

Eternal Life

∾

*"And as Moses lifted up the serpent in the wilderness,
even so must the Son of Man be lifted up, that whoever
believes in Him should not perish but have eternal life."*

John 3:14–15 NKJV

Your sacrifice, Jesus, made my new life possible. Because You gave Your life on the cross, my sins are forgiven, my past behind me. Help me live each day aware of the price You paid.

Thank You, Lord, that the eternal life You purchased for me is not only available in heaven. You work out Your life in me each day, through troubles and joys. No matter what discouragement I face, You still achieve Your eternal purpose.

I seek eternity each day, Lord, trusting that one day, I'll share unending bliss with You.

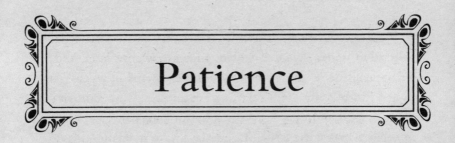

Patience

PATIENCE'S END

∽

Better is the end of a thing than the beginning of it,
and the patient in spirit is better than the proud in spirit.

ECCLESIASTES 7:8 AMP

At the end of almost anything, I'm glad when I've shown patience instead of pride. No matter what the issue, Lord, pride lands me in trouble, while patience paves the way for good things.

On my own, I have to admit I'm not very patient. Especially when I'm under pressure, I want things now, not later, and I want people to do things my way, not their own. But when Your Spirit controls my life, I relax, accept another way, and live in Your peace. Control of everything lies in Your hands.

No matter what trials I face today, make me patient, Lord.

SAFE REFUGE

∽

You [evildoers] would put to shame and confound the plans of
the poor and patient, but the Lord is his safe refuge.

PSALM 14:6 AMP

I've seen the disadvantages of patience, Lord, when others have taken advantage of my willingness to wait. I know some people see patience as weakness and foolishness.

That's not Your view. You promise that the one who takes advantage of faithful believers cannot know You as a refuge. In this time of grief, I've learned how important a shelter You are to those in pain. I can't imagine being without Your love in the middle of disaster. So I'm asking you to turn the hearts of those who confound the patient. May they come to live in You, not in their own weak plans.

Taking shelter in You is the only place to be during trouble. Thank You for being my safe refuge.

Slow Down

The thoughts of the [steadily] diligent tend only to plenteousness, but everyone who is impatient and hasty hastens only to want.
PROVERBS 21:5 AMP

Thank You for reminding me, Lord, that patience has its own deep benefits. When I want to hustle through this world, avoiding the stop lights, I seek the "good life" but miss out on Your best. Your halts along the way are intended to help me experience the best You designed for my life.

Trials that come with patience aren't fun. But blessing, not fun, has always been Your goal. My hurried pace seeks to avoid pain, setting its own pleasure-filled agenda for life. In doing so, it misses untold blessings You planned for me.

Don't let me miss Your best blessings. Slow me down to do Your will, Jesus.

Undeserved Pain

※

But if you bear patiently with suffering
[which results] when you do right
and that is undeserved,
it is acceptable and pleasing to God.

1 Peter 2:20 amp

Living in You not only gives me one joy after another, Lord, but suffering also comes my way as I obey You. I don't even have to do wrong to hurt. It's not something I understand, Jesus. The joys of Your kingdom and pain don't seem compatible, yet in Your own sacrifice they clearly draw together. Your love does not deny the reality of hurt.

I can't understand it all, but You promise that patiently putting up with undeserved pain still has a purpose. I please You when I untiringly bear each trial, however large or small.

Help me give You that joy today, Jesus.

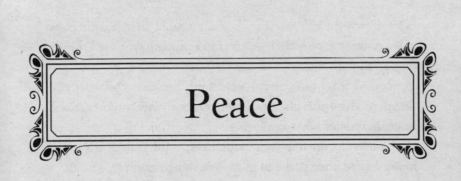

Peace

Heart Guard

∞

Be anxious for nothing, but in everything by prayer and supplication, with thanksgiving, let your requests be made known to God; and the peace of God, which surpasses all understanding, will guard your hearts and minds through Christ Jesus.

Philippians 4:6–7 nkjv

When my heart's hurting, I should pray first, Lord. How often do I remember that—or feel like praying when my mind's distracted with worry?

I can't live on painful emotions because they get me nowhere. But trust, placed in You, offers an influx of peace and hope, no matter what I'm facing.

When anxiety floods my soul, Lord, send Your Spirit to my heart. I need Your peace to guard me day by day.

Strong Peace

∞

The Lord will give strength to His people; the Lord will bless His people with peace.

Psalm 29:11 nkjv

Your peace is my strength, Lord. Without it, I am pulled in many directions, uncertain where to go or how to live. But when Your serenity fills my heart, I easily head in Your direction. I know whom I serve and where I need to go. Together we walk in the eternal way.

Thank You, Jesus, for promising me Your peace, no matter

whether I face trials or the best of times. My circumstances mean nothing, for Your blessing is larger than any earthly predicament.

Today, I need Your peace. May Your Spirit pour it out on my life so I can pass Your strength on to others.

PEACE PROMISE

But the meek shall inherit the earth, and shall delight themselves in the abundance of peace.

PSALM 37:11 NKJV

Meekness isn't very appealing in today's world, Lord. We're more likely to admire forceful people who want to go their own way. Serving You by following Your Word doesn't go far if I'm looking for general approbation.

The only approval I honestly need is Yours, Lord. I didn't become a Christian so the world would appreciate me, but because You offered me new life. You have not failed me, Jesus, because Your peace has flooded my soul as I've turned to You and obeyed Your commands.

Those of us who obey You may have yet to inherit the earth, but if this peace is a foretaste of Your promise, I know how wonderful it will be, Lord. Thank You.

UNTROUBLED

∞

"Peace I leave with you; my peace I give you.
I do not give to you as the world gives.
Do not let your hearts be troubled
and do not be afraid."

JOHN 14:27

Knowing and following You daily is nothing like living in the world, Lord. The huge divide between Your kingdom and an earthly one hardly fits into words. Anxiety fills the earth as people worry about their futures. Peace seems fleeting and doubtful. The search for rest never ends. But in Your kingdom, even Your kingdom here on earth, You give deep, restful serenity that brings me through the worst trial, the most difficult situation. When I trust in You, my heart never has to feel concerned.

Still, there are times when peace seems far from me. Turn my heart to trust in You so peace descends upon my soul.

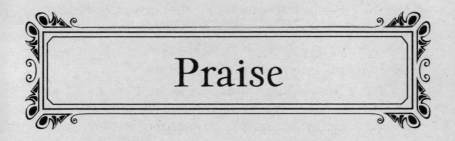

Praise

JOY IN SORROW

∞

*Light is shed upon the righteous and joy on the upright
in heart. Rejoice in the LORD, you who are righteous,
and praise his holy name.*

PSALM 97:11–12

Right now I may not feel as if joy follows me through the day or rushes ahead to prepare the way for me, Lord. But I trust Your promise will be fulfilled in the times ahead. Because today doesn't feel wonderful doesn't mean Your Word changed or You have forgotten me. Your light still guides me through the storms and leads me in Your eternal path.

Thank You for Your faithfulness to me, Lord, no matter what I feel or experience. I praise You for being there, willing to help me, no matter what I face. You are Lord!

SATISFIED

∞

*The poor will eat and be satisfied;
they who seek the LORD will praise him—
may your hearts live forever!*

PSALM 22:26

Anyone, even the poorest soul who honestly seeks You, becomes filled with Your love, Lord. You never turn away a hurting heart looking to You for salvation.

Though I've experienced Your saving grace, my heart sometimes still feels empty, Jesus. But it's never Your fault.

You offer many reasons to receive my praise; You fill me with Your love, life, and blessings. If my heart echoes with doubt, it's because I have not turned in trust to You.

I want to be satisfied with the blessings You've prepared for me, Lord, and share them with others, too. Daily turn my heart to Your truths, and help me speak Your praises to the world.

GREAT LOVE

For great is his love toward us, and the faithfulness of the Lord endures forever. Praise the LORD.

PSALM 117:2

I have a lot to praise You for, Lord, if I look clearly at my life and the blessings You've poured out on me. One sorrowful event can't close the door on all You've done for me in the past and Your continued provision for me.

Nor have You turned Your back on me in a time of grief, for as I've turned to You for comfort, You've responded generously. As I share my pain with You, Your loving Spirit fills me with comfort.

Your love has been great to me, more than I could ever deserve. I praise You for the love and faithfulness You've poured out in my life. Thank You, Jesus.

BURDEN BEARER

∞

Praise be to the Lord, to God our Savior,
who daily bears our burdens.

PSALM 68:19

You have borne this great burden for me, Lord, or I could never have gotten through the grief. Thank You for standing by me, directing my steps, and healing my pain. Every day, You've provided all I needed as I have asked for aid.

I praise You, Jesus, for taking up all my hurts so I could continue living. Without Your strength, I might have collapsed under the pain. How can I give You enough thanks and praise for Your love and faithfulness? Though I filled the world with them, I could never adequately repay You.

Help me pass on the word of Your faithfulness to others who hurt, Lord. I know they need a burden bearer, too.

Prayer

MIGHTY THINGS

❧

*" 'Call to Me, and I will answer you, and show you great
and mighty things, which you do not know.' "*
JEREMIAH 33:3 NKJV

How can I know great things if I am not willing to spend time with You, Lord? If I ignore my Creator, how can I learn of the mighty things You have done?

Forgive me, Lord, for my unwillingness to pray. Life often interferes with my prayer plans, and I end up shortchanging You. Make me faithful to my meetings with You in prayer and meditation. Give me a desire for Your Word that spurs me to spend time with You.

Thank You, Jesus, for wanting to share Your mighty things with me. I'm calling on You now so You can show me each one.

EFFECTIVE PRAYER

❧

The effective, fervent prayer of a righteous man avails much.
JAMES 5:16 NKJV

A good prayer is worth much in Your eyes, Lord. Because a Christian draws close to You in frequent prayer, You answer many petitions and benefit both the one who prays and the one in need.

In times of trouble, I've known the blessing of some fervent prayers on my behalf. When my heart agonized, I suddenly felt Your peace and knew someone lifted me up to You. Thank You for those faithful believers who remembered my need.

I also want to be an effective, fervent prayer so I can bless others who need to know You or need Your aid in trouble. Help me pass on the blessing, Jesus. So many people need it today.

Prayer Power

∽

The Lord is far from the wicked,
but He hears the prayer of the righteous.

Proverbs 15:29 NKJV

This verse fills me with awe, Lord, when I think that You want to listen to my prayers. Many call on You out of pride-filled hearts, and You cannot heed. But because I gave my life to You and want to hear Your voice, You always hear my cries.

Speaking to You in prayer gives power to my life. When I turn to You in trouble, I tap into Your strength. Though I may not get an expected answer, You often give me even more than I ask. Better responses seem to be Your specialty, Lord. So draw me close to You. When I seek the desires of Your heart, You are always listening.

BELIEF

∞

"And all things you ask in prayer, believing, you will receive."
MATTHEW 21:22 NASB

Without faith, I receive nothing from You, Lord.

At times, my faith seems so small, all I can do is ask for Your help to believe. But even that tiny seed of faith can grow a large prayer plant. You never desert me when my heart is humble enough to listen.

So even when the world seems to smash me down and my belief is small, I reach to You for help. As Your Spirit touches my heart again and I believe, I've already received the best: Your touch of new life for my spirit.

Touch me again, please, Lord. I have so little to offer You, but I am trusting You today.

Refuge

STRONG ARMS

"The eternal God is your refuge, and underneath are the everlasting arms. He will drive out your enemy before you, saying, 'Destroy him!'"

DEUTERONOMY 33:27

Your strong, everlasting arms hold me safely, Lord, even in trouble. Though I may not see them, they support me, no matter what enemy I face. Foes flee before Your face when I trust in You.

Help me believe You are always there for me, forever keeping me from harm. I want to live and trust in You, instead of falling into danger because I doubt Your care.

Hold me tight today, Lord Jesus. I need Your protection from every enemy—spiritual and temporal—that comes against me. You are my only refuge, Lord.

OUR SHIELD

"As for God, his way is perfect; the word of the LORD is flawless. He is a shield for all who take refuge in him."

2 SAMUEL 22:31

When You protect me, Lord, nothing can touch me. What arrow or sword reaches past You to the one You love? Your promises of defense do not fail.

Though I struggle or face an enemy, I still trust the battle will be won in You. Nothing before me has not already passed by You, and in You is all the strength I need to overcome my foes.

Help me walk in Your perfect way, Jesus, whether it's through fire and sword or into a perfect garden. I only want to live in Your way, where You shield me from all harm.

GOD'S JUSTICE

Submit to God's royal son, or he will become angry, and you will be destroyed in the midst of your pursuits—for his anger can flare up in an instant. But what joy for all who find protection in him!

PSALM 2:12 NLT

How deeply those who reject Jesus offend You, Lord. Repudiating Your Son, they kindle Your deep anger. It's not a picture I like to imagine, but Your Word tells me it's true. Rebellion against You fuels Your anger.

But justice, not anger, is Your nature. You seek to bring souls into Your love. Drawing those who accept the sacrifice of Your Son into Your kingdom, You protect them forever and bring them joy.

Even in trials, help me to submit to Your will, Lord. I want to live always in Your protection, so help me keep my eyes on Your eternal truths.

TASTING GOD, TASTING GOOD

∞

Taste and see that the LORD is good;
blessed is the man who takes refuge in him.

PSALM 34:8

Knowing You is such joy, Lord, that it's hard to imagine anyone rejecting You. I have tasted of Your love, Lord, and known its deep blessing.

When sorrow or doubt cross my path, let me taste again of Your goodness that turns my heart soft and pliable toward You. The depth of Your tender love bowls me over, when I consider how You have cared for me. Every time I savor it anew, I am humbled and feel blessed all over again.

Nothing is sweeter than You, Jesus. Thank You for being my refuge.

Rest

Burdens Lifted

∞

"Come to Me, all you who labor and are heavy laden,
and I will give you rest."

Matthew 11:28 NKJV

Burdened—I know the feeling, Lord. Weighed down by grief, I feel as if a heavy pack—one no human wants to lift for long—crushes my shoulders. But You, the burden lifter, are not so limited. Your Word promises You can hoist this weight from me and give me rest.

I have no one else to go to, Lord. No help on earth can ease my spirit today. I desperately need the rest You offer. The more I struggle for release, the more my burden weighs me down.

Take all my sins and doubts, Lord, and exchange them for Your peace. Fill my heart with trust in my burden bearer, and make my life whole again.

Contented!

∞

The fear of the Lord leads to life, and he who has it will
abide in satisfaction; he will not be visited with evil.

Proverbs 19:23 NKJV

This isn't a popular idea, Lord: Few people like the idea of fearing You. But You are powerful beyond anything our hearts and minds can imagine, and wise people—those who believe in You—know You deserve respect and obedience.

I need not go in fear of You, though. You have made me

Your child, and that makes all the difference. You've offered me rest in You, and I've accepted. How awesome that You no longer want my fear but my faith. In You, my heart need never dread. I'm trusting in my Lord and rest content.

ETERNAL REST

∞

[Our] faith and knowledge [rest] on the hope of eternal life, which God, who does not lie, promised before the beginning of time.

TITUS 1:2

Before time began, Lord, You promised Your faithful ones eternal rest in You. No afterthought, eternal life was planned from the beginning, if we trusted in You.

Though I have yet to see heaven, my heart cannot doubt its reality. You, the incredibly faithful Lord, have promised it, and Your promises never fail. Though my eyes may not yet see Your everlasting kingdom, faith assures me of its existence. Every day in You strengthens my knowledge of its truth.

Thank You, Jesus, for promising me this rest. On earth I experience only a taste of it, but in eternity I will eat the bread of Your kingdom forever.

REST IN GOD

∞

The LORD replied, "My Presence will go with you, and I will give you rest."

EXODUS 33:14

When Moses wanted to know more of You, You gave him this promise, Lord. I've learned the truth of it, too. When I'm close to You, I feel a deep rest. Challenging circumstances don't disturb me much when I'm at peace in You.

I don't have to lead a nation, as the prophet did. I may not be great or famous, but You still ask me to draw near and feel the calm You give. As Your child, I am asked to draw ever closer to You, day by day.

Today I need Your Presence, Lord. Help me rest in You always. Like Moses, I'm nothing on my own.

Righteousness

Faith Alone!

❦

However, to the man who does not work but trusts God who
justifies the wicked, his faith is credited as righteousness.

ROMANS 4:5

Contrary to popular belief, I can't earn my way into heaven.
You've made that abundantly clear in Your Word, Lord. But I
may still be tempted to fall into sin and then try to earn back
the things of heaven. It's hard to give up human ways and
accept the truth that all I need is faith.

Keep me unswerving, Lord, in trusting that what You say
is true. Because I've accepted Your Son's sacrifice, You count me
as righteous, though I fail You often. What I cannot do myself,
Jesus has done for me.

Thank You, Jesus, for giving me righteousness. On my own
I could never be perfect.

Faithful Servant

❦

You have been set free from sin and
have become slaves to righteousness.

ROMANS 6:18

In my own wisdom, I don't relish being a slave, Lord. Giving
up my own ways and handing authority to You does not come
easily.

But when I think of the slavery to Satan that once bound
me and still attempts to clutch at my soul, I realize how blessed

I am with freedom. Serving You, fulfilling Your righteousness on earth, is nothing like the sin slavery of the evil one.

Serving You, Lord, is such a blessing to me. Thank You for making me Your slave. Help me to be a faithful servant, too.

FILLED

"Blessed are those who hunger and thirst for righteousness, for they will be filled."
MATTHEW 5:6

Being hungry and thirsty hardly seems a blessing, Lord, until You tell me it is. Naturally, I'd rather have my life full of good things than dry and empty. But I've seen the truth of Your promise when Your Spirit has filled my dry and empty spiritual places with His power.

Instead of looking for the good things this world offers, I need to hunger and thirst for Your right ways and walk in them. Give me the desire for Your righteousness, Lord, and make me unfulfilled until it is part of my daily life.

When I am empty, Your Spirit has a space to fill. Open my life to Your work today.

PROVISION

∾

*"But seek first his kingdom and his righteousness,
and all these things will be given to you as well."*

MATTHEW 6:33

My first priority should be Your kingdom, Lord, not my lifestyle. I tend to forget You know what I must have to live. Help me remember this promise that I need not worry about life's necessities if only I put You first.

I have to admit it's a challenge to give up my old, careful ways of making sure I have "enough." It's easier to cling to money and possessions. Such a life, though full of things, creates an empty earthly kingdom, not Your blessing-filled one.

Despite my doubts, I put Your kingdom first today. Show me how to live in Your right ways. I know You will provide all I need.

Salvation

DELIVERED

∾

He fulfills the desires of those who fear him;
he hears their cries for help and rescues them.

PSALM 145:19 NLT

Deliverance lies only a prayer away for those who love You, Lord. When we need spiritual or physical help, we turn to You, and You bring us to the place we need to be.

Trouble cannot destroy Your salvation, deafen You to my cries for help, or keep You from acting. The evil one cannot deny or deter Your faithful promise.

Thank You for bringing me my desires. Already, through my obedience to Your Word, they reflect Your salvation and show my hunger to follow You. Give me the longing to follow You ever more closely, Jesus. Being Your child and working out Your saving will is such a blessing.

STRONG DEFENSE

∾

The name of the LORD is a strong tower;
the righteous run to it and are safe.

PROVERBS 18:10 NKJV

You alone are my defense, Lord; no earthly fortification compares to Your protection. When I face trouble, instead of asking, "Why me?" or complaining of the attack, I need only run to Your tower. There I find all the help I need.

Nothing else keeps me safe from spiritual harm, Father.

Deliverance cannot come from a form of religion or keeping a set of rules. Only a relationship with You keeps me for eternity.

Thank You for being my tower, Jesus. I don't want to run to anyone else. Help me run to You today as the world attacks.

SOLE SAVIOR

∞

"The man who loves his life will lose it, while the man who hates his life in this world will keep it for eternal life."

JOHN 12:25

Losing everything is scary to me, Lord. Though I know I'm part of Your eternal kingdom, this world still feels very important to me. Letting go of what I know is hard.

But You promise that losing my life will not be the disaster I imagine, because I'm living in Your eternity. Only by losing this world will I really find what I'm looking for.

Nothing in this life that is given up to You is truly lost. Please loosen my clinging hands and heart when they desire to save earthly things instead of holding on to heavenly truths. I give You my whole life, Lord, my sole Savior.

SHARED LOVE

∞

*"For God did not send his Son into the world to condemn
the world, but to save the world through him."*

JOHN 3:17

I've needed Your salvation, not judgment, in this time of trial,
Lord. How thankful I am that You have not condemned my
failings, but when I've hurt, You have drawn near.

When life has been tense, it's sometimes been easier for
me to want to judge and condemn instead of lifting up another
hurting heart. Thank You for encouraging me, instead, to pass
on the love You've shown me. You have not given me the role
of judge or savior, but I can pass on the message of forgiveness
that You gave. Help me reach out to empty hearts today and
share the love that's meant so much to me.

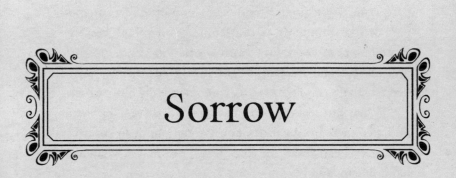

Sorrow

Good for the Heart

∾

Sorrow is better than laughter,
because a sad face is good for the heart.

Ecclesiastes 7:3

I don't like to feel sad, Lord. Hurting doesn't feel good, and part of me doesn't understand why I should suffer. But another part of me comprehends that some good things happen on those less-than-good days. Sorrow often drives me to trust in You more deeply because I can't handle life on my own. The deeper relationship that grows from pain truly blesses me.

When life seems good, it's easy to believe I have things under control. But in truth, You are the one who controls all. Make my heart aware of that, Jesus, no matter what my life looks like today.

Living Water

∾

"For the Lamb at the center of the throne will be their shepherd;
he will lead them to springs of living water. And God will
wipe away every tear from their eyes."

Revelation 7:17

One day, when all tribulations end, no tears will fall, Lord. You've promised an end of sorrow for Your faithful ones.

You've been my Shepherd on earth, caring for all my needs, and I've tasted sips of Your living water—or perhaps a cup— as I've walked faithfully with You. But one day, streams will flow abundantly throughout Your land. All will be able to drink their fill and delight fully in You.

Now, as I trust in Your promise, hope wells up. Today let me sip of Your water and live on earth trusting in Your heavenly truths.

DELIVERED

〰

For you, O LORD, have delivered my soul from death,
my eyes from tears, my feet from stumbling.
PSALM 116:8

When tears course down my face, I cannot see the joy in life, Lord. All seems dark, distressing, and empty. My humanity locks me in one painful place, and I feel as if life will never improve.

But You remind me that You delivered me from death, tears, and the ability to fall into wrongdoing. Sorrow may be a stopping place, for a while, but it is not my end. You, Lord, have delivered me, body and soul, from all that would destroy me. You've set me on the path of life, and nothing can deter Your plan.

Help me live in You, Jesus, all the days of my life. Keep my soul, emotions, and feet from paths that lead to sorrow.

GOOD SORROW?

❧

Godly sorrow brings repentance that leads to salvation and leaves no regret, but worldly sorrow brings death.

2 CORINTHIANS 7:10

Lord, You've given one purely good sorrow—the one that admits to sin and opens the door to repentance. Those who feel the weight of their sins and turn to You for relief discover the joy in life You want to share with all.

This time of loss brings me much distress, but I know I have a future hope in eternity. Many who join me in woe feel deeply but have no happy expectation to ease their burden. Their sadness remains only earthly and leads to death because they do not know You.

Though my heart aches, help me offer Your hope to those lost in sadness. Together we need to find our way in You, Jesus.

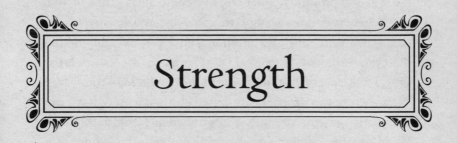

Strength

FEARLESSNESS

❈

So do not fear, for I am with you; do not be dismayed,
for I am your God. I will strengthen you and help you;
I will uphold you with my righteous right hand.

ISAIAH 41:10

I have felt fear, Lord, and dismay has attempted to overwhelm me. But You promise neither will overcome me if I trust in You.

When trust seems hard to come by, You've offered the strength of Your Spirit and reminded me that Your hands uphold me every moment. Because I've believed in the Trustworthy One, I will never fall. You never fail those who love You.

I want to live a fearless life, based on trust in You. But I can only do it with the strength You give when I hold fast. Thank You, Lord, for aiding me even at this moment. I need not fear, whatever I face today.

ONE WEAK LIFE

❈

He [Jesus] will keep you strong to the end, so that you
will be blameless on the day of our Lord Jesus Christ.

1 CORINTHIANS 1:8

Your strength doesn't last for a season, Lord. It's ever available to me because I've trusted in You. Never will You fail me. Only with Your power in me can I remain faithful to the end, despite temptation or doubt. When I do not trust in myself, but in

You, my Redeemer, I faithfully accomplish each task You place before me.

Thank You, Lord, for offering to share Your strength with me. Make me solid in You, Jesus, because on my own I am so frail. Then, as I share the truth about the source of my strength, others will begin to understand the impact You can have on one weak life.

STRENGTH IN GOD

The God of all grace, who called you to his eternal glory in Christ, after you have suffered a little while, will himself restore you and make you strong, firm and steadfast.

1 PETER 5:10

In the midst of suffering, I trust myself in Your hand, Lord. Though I cannot understand the plan for my life today, I know You are developing one that's greater than I can imagine. You've been faithful to me before, and You continue to stand by me when I face trials and troubles.

Jesus, remind me of Your suffering that brought so many benefits to my life. Through Your sacrifice, You made a way for us to meet in love. Tell me of the eternal joy we'll share once the sorrows of this world are done. And help me remain strong, firm, and steadfast when suffering touches my earthly life.

STRONGHOLD OF GOD

The salvation of the righteous comes from the LORD;
he is their stronghold in time of trouble.

PSALM 37:39

What am I trusting in to protect me, Lord? People or things of this realm cannot keep me from harm. You are the only real salvation. I've experienced this truth in my own time of trouble. When I've run to You for help, it has come, though often in unexpected ways. I appreciate all Your plans which surpass my expectations. Your protection remains a surprise, but it is always sure.

I still feel my loss keenly, but I know You're keeping me safe in Your love. And in the end, I will experience Your eternal stronghold—heaven.

Suffering

OPEN EARS

✸

"He delivers the poor in their affliction,
and opens their ears in oppression."

JOB 36:15 NKJV

When I'm in trouble, Lord, I certainly hear Your voice more clearly. You open my ears because I need to hear Your truths. I'm glad You give me an extraordinary ability to listen in the middle of pain. But Your help doesn't end there. You both listen to all my needs and deliver me from oppressive affliction.

Though I hate going through any hurt, You even give my suffering value. If anguish draws me close to You, it becomes a blessing. Thank You, Jesus, for walking through this trial and then ending it. You have both delivered me and made me know You well.

NOT FORGOTTEN

✸

For he has not despised or disdained the suffering
of the afflicted one; he has not hidden his face
from him but has listened to his cry for help.

PSALM 22:24

You, Lord, never despise Your children who are in pain. Just as You did not ignore Your Son, though He suffered on the cross, You do not ignore my hurts.

When I don't immediately receive a quick answer, remind me that Jesus' work on the cross was not quickly apparent to those who watched Him die. Though I do not get a fast response, You are not ignoring me.

Thank You for this promise to hear my cry, Lord, though it speaks through pain. I know You are with me in every trial.

OVERSHADOWED

∾

For I consider that the sufferings of this present time are not worthy to be compared with the glory which shall be revealed in us.
ROMANS 8:18 NKJV

Nothing going on in my life today is so horrible that it will not be overshadowed by the glory You provide in eternity, Lord. But it's easy to forget that truth when life presses in on me, finances are tight, or sorrow fills my heart.

I need reminding that this pain is not forever. No sad or hurtful thing I go through today lasts endlessly. But the glory You offer me through Your Son will. Fix my heart on the everlasting, Jesus, when troubles nearly overwhelm me. Nothing compares with the heavenly joy You offer.

Heart Whole

❧

For as the sufferings of Christ abound in us,
so our consolation also abounds through Christ.

2 Corinthians 1:5 nkjv

When I follow in Your footsteps, I experience suffering, Jesus. Sometimes hurts come simply because I've been faithful to You and another human doesn't appreciate that. People and situations can injure me deeply.

But You know that, Jesus, and You offer my heart deep consolation. Because I'm following in Your steps, I feel nothing You have not already encountered. The pain that lances through my heart has already passed through Yours.

Thank You for the consolation of Your Spirit, which reaches deep hurts and heals them completely. No suffering lies beyond Your touch, Lord. In You I become heart whole again.

Thankfulness

GOD'S GOODNESS

∞

Oh, that men would give thanks to the LORD for His
goodness, and for His wonderful works to the children of men!
For He satisfies the longing soul, and fills the hungry
soul with goodness.

PSALM 107:8–9 NKJV

Thank You for Your goodness and the wonderful blessings You offer all of us in this world. Your works tell of Your glory each day, but how rarely I remember to thank You for them. Forgive me, Lord.

Not only do You fill my eyes with the glory of a sunrise or the beauty of a mountain, You've also filled my empty soul with Your love. No part of my being is left untouched by wonder for Your greatness.

Thank You, Jesus, for the love and mercy that satisfy my hungering heart. Help me both to experience those truths and pass them on to other hurting souls.

HEART AND HANDS

∞

"Offer to God thanksgiving, and pay your vows to the Most High.
Call upon Me in the day of trouble; I will deliver you,
and you shall glorify Me."

PSALM 50:14–15 NKJV

Thanksgiving and obedience don't always come easily to my heart and hands. Suddenly, when I need Your help, I may wonder where You went, Lord. If my own sin distances You, You seem slow to answer.

I don't want that experience in my Christian walk, so I'm asking forgiveness for the promises I've made and not kept and the words of thanks that never crossed my lips. Thank You, Lord, for every blessing You've poured out on me, especially those I never asked for. More blessings than I requested have come my way.

Now I offer You my heart and hands; use them in Your service. Help me glorify You alone.

MERCIFUL GOD

❧

Oh, give thanks to the LORD, for He is good!
For His mercy endures forever.
PSALM 118:1 NKJV

How good You are, Lord. Not only have You saved me, Your mercy follows me throughout my days.

I fail You more often than I like to think, Jesus. Though aware of Your love for me, I still have not kept Your laws perfectly. My heart delights in Your love, yet sin tempts me, and I follow quickly.

But every day—or even every moment—You offer refreshed mercy if I simply come to You, admit my sin, and seek to obey. So I'm here today, asking for forgiveness. Thank You, Jesus, that Your mercy never fails. Keep me living in Your goodness and asking to be free from all that separates me from Your love.

VICTORY!

∞

But thanks be to God! He gives us the
victory through our Lord Jesus Christ.

1 CORINTHIANS 15:57

Thank You, Lord, that whatever battle I'm fighting will not be lost in You. Wherever faith in You leads, I follow the winning general—Jesus!

Death cannot elude or defeat You, Lord, because Your sacrifice exterminated death as nothing else could. In You lies spiritual life that overwhelms all enemies.

As You work out Your victory in my life, despite my loss, remind me the battle is not over. In eternity, all eyes will see the glorious victory You've won. Thank You, Lord, for sharing this, Your greatest prize, with me.

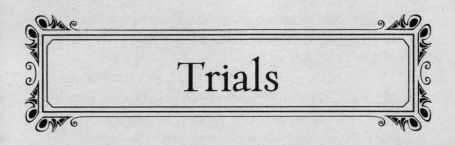

Trials

Pure Joy

❧

Consider it pure joy, my brothers, whenever you face trials of many kinds, because you know that the testing of your faith develops perseverance. Perseverance must finish its work so that you may be mature and complete, not lacking anything.

James 1:2–4

Perseverance isn't my ultimate goal, Lord. Nor is it a quality that always appeals to me, because it takes so much effort, and I don't see its value quickly. But I need it in order to become mature and complete in You.

Facing trials, sometimes I'd like to give up. But where would I go, except to You? No one else will walk with me through every moment of pain. So even in trouble, I press on, doing Your will. Keep me faithful, aware that one day I will lack nothing. Fix my eyes on eternity, when joy will be complete in You, Jesus.

Best Thing Ever!

❧

Blessed is the man who perseveres under trial, because when he has stood the test, he will receive the crown of life that God has promised to those who love him.

James 1:12

You mean I can wear a crown, Lord, simply for standing firm in the middle of trials? The closest I've come to that is a nice hat, and it isn't at all the same!

But on the day You give faithful ones the crown of life, it will be different. With a crown comes authority. No human power, but Yours will be glorified, because only with Your Spirit's work could anyone have stood for Your truths.

On that day, if I stand fast, all the troubles that came with trials will seem less than nothing. Ruling with Jesus will be the best thing ever!

Long-term Goals

In this you greatly rejoice, though now for a little while you may have had to suffer grief in all kinds of trials. These have come so that your faith—of greater worth than gold, which perishes even though refined by fire—may be proved genuine and may result in praise, glory and honor when Jesus Christ is revealed.

1 Peter 1:6–7

The faith test isn't easy, Lord, or it wouldn't be valuable. Still I shrink from pain, protecting myself as if untouched emotions should be most treasured. I ignore Your promise that my faith is more precious than gold and only trials refine it into absolute purity.

As I suffer, take my eyes from my own painless short-term goals. Put my vision instead on Your eternal end—strong faith that causes me to give You praise and honor and celebrate You as Lord of all.

KEEP TRUSTING

∾

He will call upon me, and I will answer him;
I will be with him in trouble, I will deliver him and honor him.

PSALM 91:15

All I have to do to get Your ear is call on You, Lord? If I believe, You will answer? What a wonderful promise!

In my more faithful moments, I rejoice, knowing You are at my side and will bring all this to pass. I delight in Your faithfulness. But when I face trials, it's tough to hold on to that confidence. Yet Your truth doesn't rely on how I feel. Your promises rely on Your nature, not my emotions.

Jesus, I'm thankful You are Lord and are in charge of everything. You've promised to deliver and honor me, and You will. My part is to keep trusting in You. Help me do that today.

Trust

GOD AS REFUGE

❧

It is better to take refuge in the LORD than to trust in man.

PSALM 118:8

I admit, Lord, that I have sought refuge in people, not You, and it's been an empty thing. As much as others want to help, unless they point me to You, all their kindness may be in vain. Even at their most trustworthy and faithful, people fail.

But when I trust in You, I am always safe. I can bring You my hurts, share my experiences and emotions, and no one learns my private things from You. You never betray or fail to comfort me.

I'm taking refuge in You today, Lord, instead of those around me. Touch my heart and protect me. For a time, bring me into the fortress of Your love, then send me out, strengthened, to be part of the battle for Your kingdom.

GOD'S PROTECTION

❧

The LORD is my strength and my shield; my heart trusts in him, and I am helped. My heart leaps for joy and I will give thanks to him in song.

PSALM 28:7

Standing behind You is the best place to be in a battle, Lord—and life on earth is always a spiritual battle. Daily, I pick up my sword, even when it seems to weigh me down.

But knowing You're protecting me causes my heart to leap

with joy. Who else has such a defender? None who deny You can stand behind Your shield.

Thank You, Lord, for all Your care. Today, I'm singing a song of joy that tells the world of Your faithfulness. Let my praises encourage others who are struggling in battle.

Stumbling Block

〰

As it is written: "Behold, I lay in Zion a stumbling stone and rock of offense, and whoever believes on Him will not be put to shame."

ROMANS 9:33 NKJV

I know plenty of people who have stumbled over You, Lord. Every day I meet those who deny or ignore You, offended at Your gospel. Often they're offended by my life, too, because I follow You.

When others do not understand or make my life difficult, give me compassion and words that reach their hearts and souls. I don't want anyone to miss out on Your love. As I face others' doubt and anger, remind me it's You they're really fighting. Help me believe that You will win a victory with my testimony, if only I trust in You.

MERCIFUL PROMISE

∾

Many sorrows shall be to the wicked;
but he who trusts in the LORD,
mercy shall surround him.

PSALM 32:10 NKJV

You don't promise that I'll never feel pain or suffer trials, Lord. But in not one of them will I walk alone if I trust in You. The overwhelming sorrows of the wicked will not be mine if I am faithful.

Thank You, Jesus, for Your mercy that softens or diverts every blow the world throws my way. When hardships confront me, Your mercy comforts my aching heart. As I trust in Your faithfulness, nothing overcomes me.

Your mercy surrounds me today, Lord, and I need it. Help me trust in You every minute, clinging to Your merciful promise.

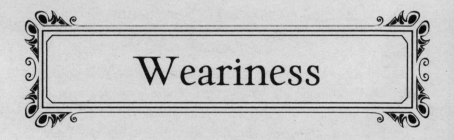

Weariness

Strength for Today

❧

Do you not know? Have you not heard? The LORD is the
everlasting God, the Creator of the ends of the earth. He will not
grow tired or weary, and his understanding no one can fathom.

ISAIAH 40:28

I'm glad that You do not grow tired, Lord, because I do. When
I feel weary, wiped out by my burdens, I need to lean on Your
strength. You, my Creator, are so much greater than I. Because I
am a weak, created being, I cannot begin to fathom Your divine
nature.

How glorious You are, Lord. I praise You for Your power
and understanding, glad You are far more powerful than I.
Thank You, Everlasting One, for reaching out to me in salvation
and letting me know Your untiring strength and wisdom. I rely
on this promise that You will never change.

Power Infusion

❧

He gives strength to the weary
and increases the power of the weak.

ISAIAH 40:29

When weariness overwhelms me, You offer strength, Lord.
If I trust You in times of frailty, despair need never win. You
have not left me powerless, though the world reinforces every
defect and removes hope from my heart. What weakness is so

strong You cannot overcome it? Could weariness overwhelm Your might? No.

I have so many weak, weary places in my heart and mind, Lord. Forgive my many doubts and wrongdoings, and infuse me with Your Spirit. When I trust in You, nothing overpowers me. Give me the strength I need to accomplish Your will today.

THE WHOLE RACE

Even youths grow tired and weary, and young men stumble and fall; but those who hope in the LORD will renew their strength. They will soar on wings like eagles; they will run and not grow weary, they will walk and not be faint.

ISAIAH 40:30–31

No human avoids weariness, Lord. You've told me that. But somehow it always disappoints me when I lack strength to accomplish my goals or give in to weakness because I'm overwhelmed emotionally. Though my mind knows this truth, I'm slow to admit my own failings.

But You have promised renewal when I hope in You. Though my situation looks dark, You're encouraging me to trust that You have all under control. In You, I overcome.

Help me soar on Your wings, run the whole race, and not faint. Only in Your strength can I find victory.

Doing Good

∞

Let us not become weary in doing good, for at the proper
time we will reap a harvest if we do not give up.

Galatians 6:9

At times, doing good, with all the energy I'm expending in my own life, seems such a strain, Lord. It's not that I want to disobey You, but I feel I lack the ability to continue. On my own, even my best intentions die, shriveled by my own lack of consistency.

When weariness wears me out, turn my heart to You again. I cannot remain strong alone—I need Your Spirit's direction and empowering if I'm going to fulfill Your will.

Thank You, Jesus, for the reward You offer those who faithfully do Your will. The harvest I reap will be all to Your glory, since I could never have done it without You.

Wisdom

WISE LIVING

❧

He who trusts in his own heart is a fool,
but whoever walks wisely will be delivered.

PROVERBS 28:26 NKJV

When I trust in my own thoughts and emotions, life always goes astray, Lord. I admit that though I seek to do right in my own power, I fail, because even my best-intentioned desires lead me in the wrong direction.

Thank You for saving me from complete failure. For when I walk in You, following Your Word and living in Your Spirit's power, I avoid foolishness. If I yield myself to Your will, wisdom fills my heart and spirit, because You work through me.

Praise You, Jesus, for all the good You bring about through my frail life. Today, help me trust in Your way, even when it's beyond my understanding. I want Your work in the world to be done through my hands.

WISE COUNSEL

❧

If any of you lacks wisdom, let him ask of God,
who gives to all liberally and without reproach,
and it will be given to him.

JAMES 1:5 NKJV

Thank You, Lord, that You don't try to hide Your wisdom or make it difficult for me to access. All I need to do is ask You for it, and You liberally provide.

My problem is, Lord, that even when You provide me with Your insight, I don't always seek to follow through. Your path isn't always easy, and my own ideas seem simpler. Though that's led me into trouble in the past, the temptation always remains to go it on my own.

Help me seek Your wisdom daily, Jesus, and follow through on Your wise counsel. It's there for me every moment, and I need to make it mine.

HEALTHY LIVING

Do not be wise in your own eyes; fear the LORD and depart from evil. It will be health to your flesh, and strength to your bones.

PROVERBS 3:7-8 NKJV

I'd like to think I'm wise, Lord, but compared to You, I'm filled with foolishness just waiting to show itself. Humility is harder to find than pride in my life.

I know Your power and wisdom, Lord. You've offered to give me all I need to follow in Your way. But my own sin gets in the way of living wisely in You.

Turn my heart to Your wisdom, Jesus, instead of my own ways. I want to live in both physical and spiritual health that are built on Your guidance and strength.

WISDOM SEARCH

∞

Happy is the man who finds wisdom, and the man who gains understanding; for her proceeds are better than the profits of silver, and her gain than fine gold.

PROVERBS 13:13-14 NKJV

What am I looking for, Lord? Have I put the pursuit of money before You, or am I dedicated to searching out Your truths?

I don't often take part in a wisdom quest, Jesus. In the excitement and pressing needs I face each day, I'm more likely to simply look for quick answers. If I had just a little more cash, I'm tempted to think, every problem would be solved.

Happiness doesn't lie in money, though. I know that when I face problems money doesn't solve them. No matter what I look for, my search always ends in You—and even if I have a money shortage, I will always be most blessed in Your love.

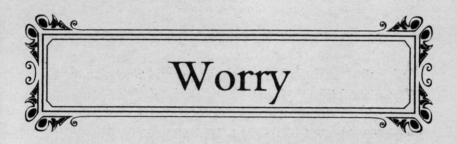

Worry

No Concern

∾

"Therefore do not worry about tomorrow, for tomorrow will worry about itself. Each day has enough trouble of its own."
MATTHEW 6:34

You know me so well, Lord. How many of my worries focus on tomorrow! Fears of things that may not even happen and concerns about others that eventually turn out right can paralyze my life.

Your words remind me I can only live in today. Tomorrow must care for itself, because looking ahead in fear wastes my days. Yet I need never worry because You control my life. No twenty-four hours, present or future, contain anything that surprises You. Nothing lies outside Your power.

When I face agitated thoughts and doubts, I need only persistently ask You to care for whatever lies ahead. Then I need no longer concern myself. Help me turn to You alone, O Lord.

Every Anxiety

∾

Cast all your anxiety on him because he cares for you.
1 PETER 5:7

No small thing in my life is unimportant to You, Lord. I can share any concern that crosses my mind because You care about it all.

I admit I have a tendency to bring You the large things sometimes. Maybe I don't want to "bother" you with my little problems. Perhaps that's how large problems come into my life: I don't deal with them when they're small by sharing them with You. Help me cast every anxiety on You, trusting that You do care and will respond. You deal with every trouble and fear, if only I ask.

Thank You for such love, Jesus. No one else helps the way You do.

LIGHTENED HEART

An anxious heart weighs a man down,
but a kind word cheers him up.

PROVERBS 12:25

Though I'm Your child, I've felt the pain of an anxious heart as I looked at the future and didn't know what would happen, Lord. I'm glad You understand the pain that comes with worry.

When a friend says a kind word, encourages me, and reminds me You are still in control of my life, my heart lightens. Knowing a fellow Christian cares, it's easier to trust You to work in my life. Words that come from Your people are often Your way of touching souls on earth.

Anxiety weighs me down, and what good does it do in the end? All my worrying and fretting won't change a thing. Trust in You makes the greatest difference. Help me stand firm in You, Jesus.

MAKE A CALL

❦

But I call to God, and the LORD saves me. Evening, morning and noon I cry out in distress, and he hears my voice.

PSALM 55:16–17

When I feel distressed, I don't have to listen to my own voice and fear that no one cares. Your ear is cocked toward my every cry, Lord. No matter what the hour, You listen to all I ask.

You not only lend an ear, you answer my cries and save me from every problem. I've seen it in the past, when problems have been solved more simply than I imagined or never really materialized at all. When I look to You in my distress, You work in amazing ways.

Thank You for Your loving response, Lord. I'm glad I made a call to You.

Yielding

Daily Cross

∞

"If anyone would come after me, he must deny himself and take up his cross daily and follow me. For whoever wants to save his life will lose it, but whoever loses his life for me will save it."

Luke 9:23-24

I'm afraid of loss of life, Lord, whether it's my own or others'. Even losing the things of this world can be hard. Yet salvation requires giving up earthly things.

Honestly, I can't say I've always picked up my cross. Sometimes I've left it at home, in a closet or drawer, when I should have held it up for You. Forgive my lapses of faith and turn me aside from the weakness and sin that caused them. Today I give my life to you again, to fulfill Your designs. Help me live in the cross and show the salvation that is already mine.

Family Blessing

∞

Be careful to obey all these regulations I am giving you, so that it may always go well with you and your children after you, because you will be doing what is good and right in the eyes of the Lord your God.

Deuteronomy 12:28

When I yield to You, Lord, obeying Your commands, I do not affect my life alone. Blessing, You promise, overflows to my children, too. Good things are never in short supply for those who love and obey You.

In times of loss, I may find obedience more difficult, but that does not mean I can't follow Your law. I should not complain that You have not given me strength to do Your will. When obedience seems impossible, I need only turn to You in prayer. The energy I need follows—and so will the joys my family will experience.

Make a blessing of my life, O Lord.

TARGET PRACTICE

≈

Submit yourselves, then, to God.
Resist the devil, and he will flee from you.
JAMES 4:7

Though others complain that the devil made them do it, I have no excuse, Lord. He cannot force me into sin, for You promised I can resist him and, in Your strength, make him flee.

Thank You, Jesus, for not leaving me in sin's clutches, unable to fight back. Yet only when I'm yielded to Your greater power will Satan's darts bounce off me. With Your Spirit filling me, I'm no longer vulnerable to his target practice.

I need Your forgiveness, Lord, and a new start today. Take all my heart and mind, and turn me only to Your will. Then when Satan throws a dart, it will not stick in me.

Standing Tall

❧

Humble yourselves before the Lord, and he will lift you up.

James 4:10

Humbling myself before anyone is difficult, Lord. I like to stand up for myself instead. But You are Lord of heaven and earth, the King of kings and wholly glorious. When I see Your power and authority, how can I fail to bend the knee?

But You do not humble me to belittle me. When I understand something of who You are and accept my own rightful place in Your world, You lift me up again. As Your child, I'm blessed beyond my expectations.

Thank You, Jesus, for lifting me again. I'm standing tall in the right place, when I'm standing there with You.

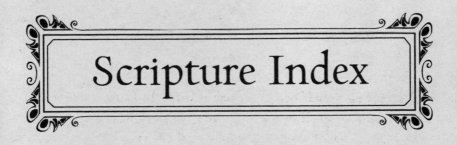

Scripture Index

OLD TESTAMENT

New Testament